TWO SISTERS & THE FOUR-LEAF CLOVER

BY SARA SHAW

Two Sisters and the Four-Leaf Clover

Trilogy Christian Publishers A Wholly Owned Subsidiary of Trinity Broadcasting Network

2442 Michelle Drive Tustin, CA 92780

Manufactured in the United States of America

10 9 8 7 6 5 4 3 2 1

Library of Congress Cataloging-in-Publication Data is available.

ISBN: 978-1-63769-728-3

E-ISBN: 978-1-63769-729-0

DEDICATION

I dedicate this book to my cousins who had the courage to relive their pain and talk out loud about their childhood abuse and how they survived. Throughout writing this book, their unselfish thoughts were steadfast about their reason for sharing about their painful past. It is their hope and mine that this might help someone else who is being abused now or has suffered abuse in their past. To tell those who are suffering to pray and believe that there is hope for a better life.

ACKNOWLEDGMENTS

Writing this book was an unexpected opportunity and blessing. Even as a young child, I had the desire to be a writer someday, but I never had the confidence to follow through. One day I happened to glance at the TV while walking in from another room. At that exact moment, there was a segment on about a Christian publishing company. My mother had recently passed away, and I was reflecting on my mom's life and how special she was, and how much I missed her. I was feeling closer to God during this time, and I was doing some soul searching. Something inside me told me that this was my opportunity. It felt right. There was a story that needed to be told. For the first time in my life, I had enough courage to take the next step.

I would like to thank my husband, Bob, who encourages me in everything I do.

Thank you to my wonderful children and grandchildren, who I love so very much, and they make my life more special every day. I am extremely proud of who they are, their accomplishments, and their talents. Their confidence encourages me to be better and try harder.

I would like to thank my friend Rhonda, who has been a rock for me. One of her gifts to me was a journal with the outside cover that read, *Work Hard, Stay Humble, Be Kind, and Take the Leap*. I took the leap.

Thank you to all the professionals in the many walks of life that have helped put things in place for me over the years: Chuck, Jackie, Tony, Chris, Sharon, Darlene, Lisa, Kay, Julie, Larry, Craig, Dan, Kerry.

Thank you to my mom, who worked hard and did her best for her family and who I love very much.

Thank you to my grandmother on my dad's side, who was my mentor and my guardian angel.

Thank you to my brother and sister for sharing many memories together.

Thank you to my longtime friend Lorraine. Our special bond covers many years.

Thank you to my brother-in-law Michael, who is an author and who encouraged me to believe in myself.

Thank you to my friends Mark and Cindy for opening their home to us.

Thank you to my cousins, my mother's sister's children.

ACKNOWLEDGMENTS

Their love, encouragement, and who they are as people have greatly inspired me. I will forever be grateful that we have been brought together.

TABLE OF CONTENTS

PREFACE

During the time of this story of the two sisters who were born in the 1930s, in this generation, while growing up at home and then getting married, the husband ruled. He was the boss. You did not question his authority. It was also at a time when it was accepted to beat children with a belt or a rubber hose, smack them, punch them, send them to bed hungry, stand them in a corner for hours because punishment taught them a hard lesson that they needed to learn. In many homes, sexual abuse was hidden from the outside world, and no one poked around asking questions. Much of the beatings and abuse left scars, deep pain, feelings of being unloved, and sometimes even hate—emotional baggage to drag around for a lifetime.

It was told to us by our mothers that they felt stuck and helpless to do anything. Both had come from an unstable home. Their mother had died when they were young, and their stepmother was a verbally hateful person. She crushed the two daughters' self-esteem. They were made to feel homely and not at all special. She kept them at odds with each other, comparing and always saying one was better than the other. After all, she would remind them both they were the homely daughters of a pig farmer—never going to amount to squat.

Through the years, the sisters persevered. Trying to figure out what love really was. A dimly lit, flickering spirit that, as they prayed and looked to God for answers, their spirit grew a little stronger as time passed on. Their desire to survive, to love their family, and to leave this world knowing they had fought to the very end. Making so many bad choices and getting a lot of it wrong but strong-spirited enough to keep going.

This is the life of those two sisters and the lives of their children that they brought into this world. They fought hard to make it better and sometimes made it worse. They fell many times along the way, but they never gave up. Their faith often waivered, and many times, they did not believe it would work out. The older sister's life, by comparison, had a better outcome than that of her younger sister, which only reinforced the wedge between them.

This story is told by Sara, who is Elizabeth's oldest daughter. Elizabeth is the oldest of the two sisters, and Evelyn is the youngest. Sara spent many days and hours with her first cousins, Evelyn's children, sharing about their childhood and life now.

Preface

Elizabeth and Evelyn left this world knowing their children loved them very much. That their children were grateful to them for all that they had sacrificed and suffered for them. They forgave them for the pain and hurt they suffered because of their bad choices and circumstances. They had to put much of this in a safe place for their own survival and ongoing search for understanding. That safe place for many of them was to believe their mothers had done the best that they could.

It is true: all things are possible with God.

Dear Lord, we thank you for being our refuge.

INTRODUCTION

It is widely and universally known that the four-leaf clover is a symbol of good luck. This symbol of being special and lucky came about because a four-leaf clover is so rare. You could search in a field full of clover, and you would be incredibly lucky and extremely fortunate to find even just one.

This incredibly special luck has been associated with what we often hear as "The Luck of the Irish."

The Irish share that there is meaning and symbolism for each leaf. One leaf for faith, the second for hope, the third for love, and the fourth for luck.

Upon hearing and believing that this all might be possibly true, one could expect to find hope and feel lucky if lucky enough to find one.

The story of the two sisters and the four-leaf clover is about their journey with many years of lost hope and what seemed to be no good luck.

It is about their children suffering sexual and physical abuse. A sister's children being taken away and put in foster care, and her fight to get them back. About being poor and sometimes going to bed hungry. A feeling that happiness was something that only other people had.

At night you could hear them crying out, "God, where are you?"

A story of being surrounded at times by such evil and darkness that one would think it would be hard to survive, so you would lose all hope and just give up. Ending your life might be better than waking up every day to repeat the same nightmare day after day.

It felt like this was their lot in life. Their destiny. Their children's destiny. Their bad luck.

Through all the pain and suffering, God's love was always there. The path was so dark it took unbelievable strength to finally find God while enduring all the pain. God's love and presence brought hope, love, and encouragement to go on.

This story will take you from the home of the two sisters growing up in a small midwestern town to the mountains of Kentucky.

So many roadblocks. So many things to overcome. But life really is what you make of it. The pain, the hurt, and betrayals make you stronger.

Mixed with much heartache and pain along the way, there were also celebrations and big accomplishments. There were successes despite the hardships. Accomplishments always felt more powerful because there were many people talking and saying that nothing good would come from any of them. Some referred to the sisters and their children as "damaged goods."

Kids at school would make fun. Some teachers even labeling them, saying, "They would never amount to much. Their clothes, where and how they lived, their one pair of shoes." Christmas presents that came from church donations you picked out for yourself. Feeling embarrassed. Feeling lesser of oneself.

Reading this journey will help others to believe for themselves that they too can overcome their past. You can achieve a better life, like a lucky four-leaf clover. You need faith in God and a belief that you deserve a better destiny. You are loved by God, and you need to love yourself.

No one really wants to hear, read, and live through a true-life story that gives us only chapters of despair and hopelessness. A sad story. This is not that story. It is a story of hope, courage, and restoration. A story about finding

God, having hope, and building a new life out of the rubble.

There are lessons within each of these chapters. Lessons that tell us to look deep into our own lives and know that if they could overcome all that they did, so can you. You can change your course of life because all things are possible with God.

For their children's part, committing some of their stories and memories to paper helps with their ongoing recovery. An every-day push forward to move past the pain. To feel deserving and believe it is possible to be hopeful about the future. To forgive the hurt and above all remember they were loved. They are loved. To be proud of themselves for their achievements, courage, and strength.

The two sisters kept their two families separated for most of their lives. Their children did not understand the why of this. Uncovering some of the possible reasons and motivations continues. Some surprising twists and turns also continue to be uncovered.

There were whispers about possible reasons, but it was not until one sister passed away and the other was suffering in a nursing home from Alzheimer's that the children connected. A door was opened, and a light was turned on.

INTRODUCTION

Three boys and seven girls. Their stories bring to life the journey that has shaped their lives and the dark secrets they kept.

CHAPTER ONE

THE SISTERS

The oldest sister Elizabeth was born at her parents' home in the late, extremely hot summer of 1932. Her baby sister, Evelyn, was born two years and eight months later.

Their father was a pig farmer, and their mother was a homemaker. Their mother was seventeen, and their father was nineteen when they married. Their modest farm was in an exceedingly small Midwest Ohio town with a total population of about 850 men, women, and children.

The sisters were both beautiful babies with lots of dark curly hair and gorgeous complexions.

Many of our history books tell us when the pioneers and settlers were moving west during the 1700s and 1800s, they moved their belongings, but they also moved their pigs with them. As they started to settle and establish themselves in different towns across the west, they began to set up their pig farms and the processing facilities to process their pork.

Actually, Ohio became one of the major providers of pigs in the 1800s. Their distribution extended all the way to the east coast. Railroads greatly boosted business, providing for the transportation of pigs and processed pork. This transportation advancement provided great opportunities and bright dreams for their futures. It opened the door to wider expansion and the possibilities of great wealth.

Cincinnati, Ohio, which borders Kentucky along the Ohio River, was the epicenter for the development of the modern industrial pig industry. Ohio was a most important state for pig farming which is another reason their parents felt this to be a good opportunity. They felt they were at the right place at the right time owning and managing one of the best possible money-making opportunities for their family.

Things progressively worsened, and on October 24, 1929, it happened, "Black Thursday." Extremely nervous worried investors panicked and began selling overpriced shares.

Five days later, on October 29 was "Black Tuesday," panic was rampant, and it was the darkest of days. Wall Street and millions of shares were worthless. Investors who had borrowed money and bought stocks "on margin" were wiped out and destroyed.

Factories began firing employees. Foreclosures and

repossessions were rampant. Panic and chaos loomed all about, and people were terrified. They were in shock. Most were frozen in fear and disbelief. How could this happen?

Prayers could be heard from loud, shaky voices. "Please, dear God, help us. Please, we do not know what to do. Please save us, dear Lord."

By 1930, four million Americans could not find work, and that number grew to six million by 1931. Herbert Hoover was the president. Many Americans had lost complete hope. Many Americans blamed Hoover and his policies.

During the early years of the depression, livestock prices had dropped considerably. Government officials concluded that farmers were over-producing hogs, and that is what caused the prices to drop. The Agricultural Adjustment Act of 1933 was rolled out to reduce the supply. The "emergency livestock reductions" were then launched in the spring of 1933. Six million hogs were purchased from extremely nervous and frantic farmers.

Shockingly, all these hogs and cattle were killed. Not for food. Thousands were killed and buried in pits. Farmers did not want this at all. There were people going hungry. How did this make sense? It was hard to make sense of any of it. It went against everything they believed, but they were faced with no other choice. The federal buy-out program saved many of them from being forced into bankruptcy.

Their mother, Clara, and their father, Henry, were unable to escape the downturn in livestock prices with the recession, and they lost their farm and their only income. My mom, Elizabeth, was almost three years old, and Evelyn was soon to be born.

Their parents packed up their belongings and moved further north in Ohio in hopes of finding work there. Their father, Henry, was able to find a job with an auto manufacturer working in the machine shop. Even though wages were low and food had to be rationed, they were grateful for what they had.

Bread lines and soup kitchens are pictured in many of our history books. I remember like it was yesterday, sitting next to my mother as a little girl and her showing photographs and explaining how hard and sad this time was. I remember she thought it was important to share about what she lived through to help put into perspective how my life as a child and my siblings compared. We, too, had incredibly sad times when we were small children. She would take us aside when we thought life was hard because there was not much food or our shoes were torn and old. We have all heard the stories about "I had to walk a mile to school." There were no school busses. It is true that their lives, and for so many others during The Great Depression, were extremely hard.

Such a sad time. My mom would start to tear up when she spoke about it, and she often would say that they were surrounded by despair, hopelessness, and fear every day. They prayed morning, noon, and night.

During this time, droughts hit the Southern Plains to add to an already bad situation. High winds and dust storms blanketed, choked, and covered the states from Texas to Nebraska. Many people died. It killed livestock and destroyed crops. This tragic event was later called the "Dust Bowl." It drove desperate people and families from their homes and fleeing into the cities hoping to find work, any work, and to escape the nightmare that they left behind.

By the fall of the 1930s, there was an excessively big panic brewing in the banking business. Most investors were getting nervous and did not trust the overall financial situation. Deciding to act, the investors demanded cash which forced the banks to liquidate their loans. By the fall of 1932, thousands of banks had to completely close their doors for good. Something you would think that could not ever happen.

The Great Depression was steeped in poverty, unemployment, hunger, and hopelessness. For criminals, however, they found this to be an exceptionally good time to take advantage of the situation. It was during this Prohibition era that organized crime and other criminals thrived with bootlegging, bank robberies, murders, high-interest loans or loan sharking, and more.

This time in history, 1932, goes down and is recorded in the history books as the countries deepest and darkest of times. The Great Depression era. Over fifteen million people were unemployed. Hoover was finally out, and Franklin D. Roosevelt became the president. He had won by a landslide. The country needed change. They needed a lifeline. They needed hope and a whole lot of prayer, and a stronger faith in God. By the fall of 1932, baby Elizabeth was one month old.

By Inauguration Day (March 4, 1933), every US state had ordered all the banks that were still open to close immediately. The US Treasury did not have enough cash to even pay all their government employees. It was a very scary and uncertain time. It was at this time that FDR tried to show calmness and hope to turn down the temperature. This was when he shared those famous words, "The only thing we have to fear is fear itself." He often broadcasted over the radio waves what he called "Fireside chats." People looked forward to those broadcasts. Any words of hope and a better future were desperately needed.

The Great Depression continued to drag on through the end of the decade. Those years were 1929–1940.

By the end of 1940, Elizabeth, my mom, was eight years old, and Evelyn was five. My mom said she knelt by her bed at night, praying so long that she had deep creases in her knees.

I was really surprised to learn that pigs are the reason and how Wall Street got its name. As it turns out, during the 1600s, both feral and domestic pigs were devastating and destroying farmer's crops on Manhattan Island. Something had to be done. To put a stop to this, farmers joined together to build a wall along the island that included the street and avenue. The protective wall they built in that area thus became known as "Wall Street."

CHAPTER TWO

THE GREAT DEPRESSION AND WAR

All the hardships caused by the Great Depression era were fiery fuel for the political extremists across Europe. This was frighteningly true in Germany and Adolf Hitler's Nazi regime. Hitler had been appointed the German leader on January 30, 1933. With Hitler as the Nazi leader, the war he strategically waged broke out in Europe in 1939.

On September 1, 1939, Germany invaded Poland, which is marked and recorded as what initiated the real start of the war.

Here at home in the US, no sooner did the Depression era start winding down and coming to a long-awaited end when suddenly and unexpectedly, World War II violently hit our very own shores.

The Japanese carried out a well-planned attack on the US at Pearl Harbor in Hawaii on December 7, 1941. This forced America to immediately rise up and want to fight back to defend their country. This attack initiated the United States to go to war against Japan.

Our nation's factories went back into full production. They had to; we were at war. There was a mandatory sign-up for the military; it was called conscription, which began in 1942. The Great Depression had ended at last, and the United States had turned its full attention to this very global conflict. The infamous and deadly World War II.

In April of 1943, the sister's mother, Clara, died at the incredibly young age of just twenty-nine. She had suffered from pulmonary TB and slowly slipped away.

At the time, my mother, Elizabeth was eleven years old, and Evelyn was eight.

Shortly after their mother's death, their father started seeing another woman. From memory, the sisters both claimed that they thought it was just a few short weeks after they buried their mom. They also thought this woman might have been at their house even before their mother died. Their aunt, their mother's sister, thought this to be true.

Their dad remarried the following June of 1944. The sisters now had a stepmother. Her name was Mildred.

One of her first motherly lessons was to teach the younger sister Evelyn what it was like to be locked in a chicken coup. Evelyn had not wanted to help with the feeding of the chickens, so as punishment, she was locked in the dark, loud, very smelly, and very scary chicken coup. There were lots of these types of lessons for both of the girls as they grew up.

On June 6, 1944, our allied forces landed on the beaches of Normandy, France. This was the largest amphibious military operation in our country's history: the codename was Operation Overlord. Along with our many allies, it was a successful planned invasion of German-occupied Western Europe. It is known as D-Day.

Not quite a year later, on April 5, 1945, units from The Third Army were the very first Americans to discover a camp with thousands upon thousands of prisoners and corpses. The horrors uncovered that day still haunt many of us, even years later.

Graphic stories were printed in the newspapers. Local theatres showed newsreel pictures for the public that authentically showed the ugly truth and horrifying proof of the German torture and atrocities. This was The Holocaust.

Years ago, I remembered reading the book *The Diary of Anne Frank*. I was deeply shocked and glued to the pages as I read. Anne Frank had received a diary on her 13th birthday. It was at this age that she and her family, who were Jewish, had to flee from their home in Amsterdam and go into hiding from the Nazis. For the next two years, Anne, along with her family and another Jewish family, lived in an attic in an old office building. Her strong courage was so inspiring. She was hungry, lonely, and lived in constant fear. Every day, the threat of death was real for her if she and her family were found by the Nazis.

In August of 1944, an unknown person informed the Nazis about these two Jewish families hiding in a warehouse. They arrested both of the Jewish families and the Christian family that was helping to hide them. Anne and her sister were shipped to Auschwitz's death camp in Poland. In the fall, they were moved to Bergen-Belsen concentration camp, where the two sisters died from typhus in February of 1945 because of the deplorable conditions there. It was heartbreaking to know that less than two months later, the Bergen-Belsen concentration camp was liberated by the British. Two months too late for Anne, her sister, and so many others. Her story has always had a huge impact on me for her strong courage. For all that she suffered and the suffering and death of so many other Jewish people, families, and children.

On April 12, 1945, two generals, George Patton and Omar Bradley and the president of the United States, Eisenhower, entered the prison camp at Ohrdruf. What they found was beyond shocking. Thousands of naked dead bodies and numerous torture devices. A butcher block was used to pound out of the mouth of the dead, their teeth for their gold fillings. Eisenhower said to the world, "We are told that the American soldier does not know what he was fighting for; now, at least he will know what he is fighting against."

Eisenhower called the press back home to inform them of what they had witnessed and seen at Ohrdruf. Ohrdruf was part of the Buchenwald concentration camp network. Joseph Pulitzer organized other journalists to travel and witness and report for themselves the deadly concentration camp. Before their arrival, the journalists were saying they were skeptical and felt that the descriptions they had been hearing were blown way out of proportion. However, after arriving at the camp, Pulitzer said that everything he had thought about the stories before going was a grossly huge understatement of what the situation really was.

Congressional members came, more journalists and photographers came. Those who had already seen combat battle death said that what they saw at the camps shocked and horrified them. It could be compared to a horrible nightmare that you would never forget. They had never witnessed or seen anything like this before.

On April 15, Edward R. Murrow, an American broadcast journalist, spoke frankly to the radio audience and described the gruesome piles of dead bodies, starving tattooed children, and other horrors found within the Buchenwald camp. Men, women, and children gathered around their radios for the broadcast. Murrow called it a mild account and went on to say, "If I have offended you by this rather mild account of Buchenwald, I am not in the least sorry."

The war continued.

On August 6, 1945, the US dropped an atomic bomb on Hiroshima, Japan.

On August 9, 1945, the US dropped an atomic bomb on Nagasaki, Japan.

On September 2, 1945, the war finally came to an end. The Japanese signed surrender documents on board the battleship USS Missouri in Tokyo, Japan.

Still to this day, this time in history, World War II is the deadliest of wars. Eighty-five million lives were lost.

After the bombing of Hiroshima and Nagasaki, the Eisenhower administration distributed to families that lived in the suburbs literature on how to protect themselves from an atomic bomb. Families started building fallout shelters and stocking them with supplies. There was a lot of international tension. The worry of suffering the effects of an atomic bomb was a major concern for people. The world had seen the death and devastation from the bombings of Hiroshima and Nagasaki. It was unbelievably terrifying that this could possibly happen.

Elizabeth was thirteen, and Evelyn was ten, and this is the world they were growing up in.

So far, the sisters have lived through the worst depression and the deadliest war. The worst of the worst. They have seen the devastating pictures and the effects of two atomic bombs spreading major death and destruction. They suffered the loss of their mother. They endured hurt and mostly verbal abuse from their stepmother. The horrific pictures, radio broadcasts, and newspaper articles about the Holocaust and the brutality and murder of so many Jews.

One must wonder for those two little girls; how did they make sense of it all? They must have thought, *What kind of world are we living in?*

Two Sisters & The Four Leaf Clover

How did all these years of sadness, loss, and death shape their thinking about life? How did this shape their futures? Their life choices? I wish I would have asked my mom more questions about her life. I am sure there was much more she could have told me and my siblings about her childhood. I am sure there was much more that Evelyn could have told her children too.

Through all this, their prayers never stopped, even though their hope grew fainter. They still found time to giggle and laugh and pretend that things were not as bad as they were.

There was one bright and hopeful day that my mom, Elizabeth, talked about. A day she walked more than a mile down the road where she knew of a huge field of clover. Her plan for this incredibly special day was to search for and find a lucky four-leaf clover.

She looked up to the heavens and spoke directly to God, and said, "Please, dear Lord, help me to find a lucky four-leaf clover. Help me so I can bring luck for me, my sister, my dad, and the whole wide world."

Amen!

CHAPTER THREE

THE SISTERS LEAVING HOME

Both Elizabeth and Evelyn enjoyed school, especially high school. Even though they were three years apart, they shared a lot of the same interests. They even shared a best friend. Living in a small town, the school was also small, so just about everybody knew each other, including friends and families. Their total class size averaged about ten to twelve per grade level.

My mother, Elizabeth, the oldest sister, was a cheerleader, and so was their best friend, Naomi. Naomi came from a family of two boys and three girls. Going over to her house after school was always one of the best parts of their day. There were no strict rules at their house. There was plenty of hugs, love, praise, and affection. Plus, it was fun. Fresh baked and still warm right out of the oven, homemade chocolate chip cookies. Elizabeth and Evelyn's home life was nothing like this. Naomi's parents showed all the kids lots of positive attention, praise, affection and even spoiled their children a little bit. It became an after-school regular for the sisters to hang out there as much as possible. They would only start to pack up their book bags to head home when they both knew it was time to get going, or they would be in big trouble when they got home.

Naomi's oldest brother Daniel had a noticeably big crush on my mom, Elizabeth. He would always try to do things he thought might impress her. Things like pushups and flexing his muscles. Playing tackle football, running races, carrying heavy objects to show how strong he was. Doing tricks on his bicycle. He was about seven years younger than her, so no matter how hard he tried to impress her, she just thought he was annoying.

Both Elizabeth and Evelyn were miserable growing up in their home. There were hard slaps in the face, objects thrown at them, name-calling, belittling the girls, and crushing their already bruised egos. They were made to feel ugly all the time. They were told their teeth were too big when they smiled, flat-chested, not very bright, and many other hurtful insults. Their stepmother would lie or exaggerate a story to their father to get them in trouble. The punishment given and doled out was never tough enough to satisfy their stepmother. When one horrible deed was told to their dad about what supposedly happened, and their punishment was given, Mildred was already plotting and getting ready for the next thing she could get them in trouble for.

In their prayers each night, they told God how much they loved and missed their mom. They prayed that God would watch over them and help them to be stronger and to help make all this better.

A verse from Elizabeth's bible that was marked prominently was Isaiah 41:10, "So do not fear, for I am with you; do not be dismayed, for I am your God. I will strengthen you and help you; I will uphold you with my righteous right hand."

Both sisters talked, planned, and dreamed about getting married and leaving home. They had visions of white picket fences, lush green lawns, apple pie in the oven, picnics in the park. Freshly washed laundry hanging outdoors in the summer breeze. All they needed to do was find their prince charming, set the date, and live happily ever after.

With both Elizabeth and Evelyn in high school, they spent a lot of time fantasizing about who they should choose for a boyfriend who would also make a perfect husband. It did not take long before both had narrowed down their choices. They both felt they had found the man of their dreams.

It is important to keep in mind that this was a small school with a small student body. It would be a safe guess that because of the size of the school that perhaps the estimated average of possible husband candidates might have been about four or five. Also, to be considered is the likely possibility that some of the husband options were already taken by other girls in their class.

Elizabeth went for a tall guy with a muscular build, light complexion, and a great smile. He came from a well-known family in town who also ran a business there. His name was Owen.

Evelyn went for Mr. Dreamy. His name was Billy. He was the Elvis Presley type. He had dreamy, good looks and was very charming. You would have thought she had won the Big Prize. All the girls in school were drooling over his good looks, talking about him in the bathrooms and study halls. Drawing a big heart on paper with his name and theirs. The other girls were jealous that Billy gave Evelyn a go-steady ring.

Besides Billy's good looks, he also could play the guitar and had a singing voice, it was told, to sound like George Jones.

Things were getting progressively worse at home, and

both girls finally came to the point that they no longer wanted to live with their dad and stepmother. This situation at home accelerated the plan for getting out of the house. The only plan that made sense to them was to fall in love and get married.

With this get-out-of-the-house marriage plan on the top of their minds, it was easy for both sisters to feel like they truly had fallen madly and deeply in love. Their knights in shining armor had come to their rescue. At age sixteen, Elizabeth married Owen. Evelyn, a few years later, at age seventeen, married Billy.

The sisters felt lucky and in love. This was a four-leaf clover wish come true for them.

Neither of them was able to graduate with their high school class. Not because they were pregnant. The school policy for girls back then stated that if you were married, you were not allowed to attend school. The school did not want you associating with classmates in the classroom or in the girl's locker rooms. The concern was the possibility that they would talk about personal marital bedroom talk. It was felt that this could potentially negatively affect other female students.

My mom, Elizabeth, was nineteen years old when I was

born. My parents named me after my dad's mother, Sara Ann. I was just Sara. Three years later, my mom had a baby boy, and they named him Andy. Four years later, they had a baby girl that they named Lynn. My mom and dad, Elizabeth and Owen, were married for twenty-two years.

Evelyn married Billy on June 9, 1952. They were married for ten years and had a total of seven children. Their first child, a daughter, Katie, was born in 1953. Their first little boy, born in 1954, died from pneumonia at only seven months old. A daughter Nancy was born in 1956, a son Max was born in 1957, a daughter Maria was born in 1958, a daughter Cynthia was born in 1960, and a daughter named Mary was born in 1963. Two boys and five girls.

CHAPTER FOUR

ONE OF THE WORST DAYS IN MY LIFE

Soon after being married, the fairy tale life my mom, Elizabeth, thought she was going to have fell short of her expectations. Owen, my dad, had a bad temper and seemed to get angry with just about everything. He also liked to frequent the bars in their small town, and when he came home drunk, he would pick a fight. The fight he would pick could be about anything he could think of. It seemed, at times, it was more about showing who was the boss and who ruled. It could be a dish towel that was not hung right. The table was not wiped clean enough. Laundry had not been put away neatly enough. My dad said mean personal insults, too, that were extra hurtful for my mom because of all the mean insults that both she and her sister had grown up hearing from their stepmother. Elizabeth was suffering further abuse and attacks from her husband Owen on an already bruised and very shaky ego because of her childhood.

It was hard for her to understand because Elizabeth, my mom, said she was a good wife. She was attentive and loving to Owen and worked hard at almost everything she did to please him and to really try and make him happy. She was not afraid of hard work. She was a good cook. Her homemade pies and tasty flaky crust could have received top awards at any bake sale. She did not shy away from learning anything new. She kept herself looking good. She wanted him to still feel and be attracted to her.

As the namesake of my father's mother, Sara Ann, I was told by all his family, including my aunts and uncles, that I was deeply loved and favored. I was the first grand-daughter. I was also often told about my stubbornness and strong determination. Both my mother, Elizabeth, and grandmother, Sara Ann, were headstrong, and I inherited that trait from them.

Three years later, Elizabeth and Owen were expecting again, and they had a son. They named him Andy. A year after that, another daughter came along, and they named her Lynn.

All three of us children were strong-spirited, much like their mother and grandmother.

Soon it became very necessary for Elizabeth to find a job outside of the home to help with all the household bills. Owen was demonstrating some serious health issues and started having seizures which rapidly became more frequent and stronger. For him working and staying on the job was becoming a huge and growing issue. Now they had three children to feed and clothe, so times were getting tougher. Sometimes food was scarce, and they felt pressure trying to meet household expenses.

Owen's health issues were a real blow to his ego. Understandably, it was extremely hard for him to accept. It was most important to him to be seen and recognized as the strong and important man of the house. He strongly felt that he had to be the provider for his wife and children. Because of this, he grew increasingly angry and started becoming mean to everyone around him. This included not just his wife and children. It also included his mother, brother, neighbors, and anyone around him. Along with his meanness, his health continued to worsen. The seizures increased in intensity and more often.

Us children were being whipped with his belt, slapped, and made to stand in the corner for hours for even the very slightest reason. All the while yelling while in the corner for sometimes hours to keep our nose directly in that corner, as we sobbed, or he would beat us again. Many times, when he had whipped us with his belt, when our mother came home from work, we were made to pull down our pants to show our mother our belt marks and tell her that we had been bad kids that day.

Or if we were in the bathtub getting ready for bed without any supper, our mother would be told to go in the bathroom and just see how bad we were. To look at the belt marks on our legs and buttocks.

I remember thinking to myself, *Mom, please help us. I do not think we are that bad. Cannot you see how wrong this is? Whatever he thinks we did that was so bad, surely, we could not have deserved such a horrible beating. I have friends I talk to that are not treated this way. Mom, please help this to stop.*

We children were being punished for almost everything. One time it was for making noise while he was on the phone. My brother and sister were playing, giggling, and laughing. When he got off the phone, he beat me for not keeping them quiet. The punishment given always seemed far too harsh for the wrong-doing.

If you did not eat all the food on your plate, this was one of the big offenses in our house. Not cleaning up your plate, which meant eating all your food, was not, in the slightest, even an option. You would sit there until every crummy, cold, sometimes petrified crumb was gone. I do know that lots of other kids heard from their parents too about the starving children in the world who would be thankful for this food. You could not argue that. I am sure this is still being said and, in fact, it is still true. But I really do not like liver no matter how hungry I am. And if I could have wrapped up my cooked smelly liver and mailed it to them, I would have done so in a heartbeat.

Evelyn's married life was not what she thought it was going to be either. Her husband Billy lied about his age to get a job working on the railroad. He made good money, but on Friday, when it was pay-day, he went straight to the bar after work. He stayed drinking there until it closed all the while his wife and kids were waiting for their daddy to come home. Their dad was a drunk and a womanizer. Sometimes he never made it home over the whole weekend.

It has been often said in the small town where they lived that it is hard telling how many children he may have fathered. He was quite popular with the ladies. At last estimate, it was thought to be at least nine.

None of his kids really knew their father. He was never around much. The oldest daughter Katie told the story that one day he said he was going out for a pack of cigarettes, and he did not come home until two weeks later.

On one of his alcoholic drinking binges, he caused a horrible car crash that tragically killed the people in the other car that he hit. He was drunk, way over the legal limit, and he ran a red light and hit and killed them.

He was arrested, then charged, and went to court. He was found guilty and was sentenced to the state penitentiary for manslaughter. In fact, over the course of his life, he had numerous arrests and more jail time for drunk driving and driving without a license.

When Billy went to jail, Evelyn had five little mouths to feed. They were poor, hungry, and sad. Her oldest daughter remembers her mother taking flour and water and mixing it together to make a gravy to feed her kids. She felt the gravy might fill their little tummies with a little more substance because they would cry to her, "Mommy, I am so hungry."

Her father and stepmother were not much help. From memory as the children remember, not much help at all.

Evelyn had no choice; she had to find work with Billy in jail. But she had a big dilemma. She had no one to help watch her five children.

Sadly, of course, no one offered. It appears, and it is

deeply felt, that no one really cared.

There was a small hotel across the street from their poor little house. She thought about it and felt this was her only option, so she applied for the night shift there. Her thought was, if she fed the kids and then put them to bed, then waited until they were sound asleep, it would be safe to walk across the street and go to work. After all, she knew she could see the house from the motel. It was directly across the street.

This plan did seem to be working, and there was never a close call or emergency. The kids were asleep when she left, and she made sure to be off work and back home before they were awake. She was putting food on the table for her five children. She was managing the best that she could.

But Billy's sister, who had never liked Evelyn, wanted to make trouble for her. She found out about her job. Even though it might hurt the kids, she obviously did not care. She turned Evelyn into the authorities as an unfit mother.

The police came, they arrested her, and she was charged with contributing to neglect and distribution to delinquency.

Unfortunately, Evelyn was also pregnant at the time with her sixth child with her husband, Billy.

Two Sisters & The Four Leaf Clover

For her day in court and sentencing, her five small, scared children were just outside the courtroom doors. They were being watched over by a couple of social workers.

Evelyn was sentenced to eighteen months in the state penitentiary. The guards took her away right after sentencing. The older of the five little children never got to speak in court on their mother's behalf. None of the children were allowed to see her one last time, to hug her. Nor did she get to see and hug them and tell them that she loved them. To reassure and promise them that she would see them again.

The judge nor the courtroom ever saw their sad little faces.

The children were between the ages of three and ten. They were frightened, confused, and brokenhearted; their mommy was being taken away from them. The year was 1963.

There were no aunts, uncles, parents, cousins, or any relation that stepped up and offered to help.

That was then, and still is today, an extremely hard pill to swallow. No one cared enough or loved them enough to take them in. No one even checked on them while they were in foster care. They felt unloved and without any value.

Evelyn had the baby while in jail. It was a baby girl.

She named her Mary.

The state ordered that she had to make a choice. She could give this baby up for adoption, and if she agreed to do so, she could keep her five other children. Or she could keep this baby, and her other five children would then be adopted out, and she would no longer be able to have custody of them or see them again. She chose to give her newborn baby up for adoption. What a sad decision to be forced to make.

The day their mother was sentenced, the children were split apart by the social workers and dropped off at different foster homes in the area.

This was a shocking and another awful and terribly hard thing for the children to have to suffer through. The children had never been separated from each other. Now suddenly, without any explanation or level of comfort, they were hauled off. All five children were screaming and crying and begging not to be separated from each other. It was already traumatic being separated from their dad, their mother, and now they were being separated from each other.

This could have been seen as one of the worst days in their life. But sadly, not even close. Their nightmare had truly just begun.

CHAPTER FIVE

MY FOUR-LEAF CLOVER

As I remember this day, I cannot say for sure just exactly how old I was. What I remember most is a little girl named Sara, who was always in search of hope. Hope that things could be better. But if I had to take a guess at my age, my guess would be a little girl of maybe around eight or nine years old.

A summer-tanned little girl with a skinny, messy ponytail dressed in shorts and a top that did not match. Most likely an outfit out of a rag bag or hand-me-down bag. A little girl tattered on the outside but on the inside, full of energy and hope.

I grew up in a small town with a population at that time of maybe about 500. A railroad town with at least three or four bars, two small grocery stores, and two churches. I went to the church closest to our house. That is because I could walk there on my own because mom and dad did not go to church.

At this church, the pastor preached fire and brimstone. Every Sunday night, I was at the alter asking for forgiveness because I felt sure I was going to burn in hell if I did not repent, and I was always sorry for something.

Our house was a very modest home with nothing special about it. Old used furniture, mismatched dishes, a tiny TV, wallpaper that did not match anything, and rag rugs. I lived there with my mom and dad, brother and sister, and I was the oldest child. Being the oldest child had at least one advantage when it came to taking a bath. Bathing was only allowed once a week at our house, and bathwater was saved and shared starting with the oldest child first.

I would spend hours on the weekend and after school faithfully searching in the backyard of our house for a lucky four-leaf clover. My hope was that the four-leaf clover was going to bring us good fortune and solve the sadness in our home because of the lack of money. My father was sick and could not hold a job.

I have a very vivid memory of times when there was no food on the table. If it had not been for my grandmother and my great-grandmother, life would have been desperately worse. Sometimes a jar of my great grandmother's homemade jam on a slice of bread was a prayer answered.

So, my dedicated search for a four-leaf clover was a labor of love and my contribution to help my family.

I remember looking for hours upon hours in the backyard trying to find a lucky four-leaf clover because I believed, oh how I believed with all my heart and without the slightest doubt, that if I could only find it, our whole world would change. Our life would be better. No more abuse. No more hungry nights, no more sadness in our home.

Then finally, an incredibly special day. I remember the excitement. I finally found a real four-leaf clover. I can still see and feel the big smile on my face because I was so excited. My eyes lit up big and bright, and I could not wait to go inside the house and to announce to everyone that we had nothing to worry about anymore because I had finally found the four-leaf clover that was going to make all the difference in the world for all of us. I knew they would all be so relieved and happy.

I ran across the yard with the clover in my right hand, and as I reached the steps of the back porch, I leaped up and reached for the door handle to open the door. Just as I opened the door, the clover slipped out of my hand and fell between the crack that was between the concrete porch and the house. My heart sank, and I was in total disbelief. It was now lost forever.

To this day, whenever I see a bed of clover, my first instinct is to fall to my knees and search. To not get up until I find that lucky one. What if I had not dropped it? And since I did drop it, what did that mean? Life was so hard then, so sad, and most days seemed hopeless. The belief and the power that I gave to finding that four-leaf clover helped me to get by every day. That day I dropped the clover, I was devastated and left with a strong sense of hopelessness.

Going forward in life, the experience of the lost four-leaf clover helped me to get through some tough times. I learned that you must press on, never stop believing, having faith in God is what is most important. To hold on tight to things that are important because life can change in an instant.

I learned that hope comes from having God at your center.

My God is my protector, my everything. He pulled me up at one of the lowest times in my life when I did not want to live anymore. Tired, scared, and defeated, without hope, and trying to figure out the best way to end my life.

God looked down on me and spared my life. He showed me my life has a purpose. He quieted the fear and breathed hope and new life into me.

God, you are my savior, my strength, my rock, my clover.

There was something else going on at that time that I did not know about. While I was praying and searching for hope, love, and worthiness. While I was searching for that special four-leaf clover to save the day. What I was completely unaware of was just how bad life was for my five little cousins. Evelyn's children, my mother's sister's children. My five cousins that I never knew much about.

What I know now, and I grieve deeply and even feel sick about, is that all the while that I was focusing on how hard our lives were for us living at home, they had it far worse than we did. What I know now is, my awfully hard life did not even begin to compare with the pain, suffering, and evil cruelty my cousins suffered, and some nearly died from.

Our cousins wanted to visit my mother, their aunt Elizabeth, who they knew was suffering from Alzheimer's before she died. It was after that visit that we began some of the hardest conversations you could imagine about their lives. About our purposely planned separation from each other. Secrets were uncovered. Doors that had been closed for a long time were opened. I was finally hearing the truth about the abuse they suffered and the desperation they felt each and every day. The hurt they felt, thinking no one cared enough to save them.

My cousins and I pray every day for continued strength and bonding that will help to keep us together for the rest of our days. To help us to heal. To always be there to help heal others who are suffering now or who have suffered. God has a purpose for each of our lives, and each of us wants to share our story and help others.

So many Bible stories come to mind about suffering and being surrounded by evil.

The stories in the Bible about Jacob, Job, David, and Jesus. They went through some of the darkest of times, betrayals, and suffering. But God brought them through it all.

CHAPTER SIX

THE YEAR 1963

In the year 1961, John F Kennedy took office as our 35th president of the United States. He was our country's youngest United States president to be elected. His famous inaugural speech is etched in our memories as the president who said, "Ask not what your country can do for you—ask what you can do for your country." As our new and hope-inspiring president, he gave us reassurances that he would keep his campaign pledge to get America growing and moving again. He launched an economic movement for the country that started some of the biggest and longest expansions since World War II.

There was a feeling of hope for the whole country. It was felt at home, in the classrooms, and on the TV and radio broadcasts we listened to and watched with our families from home. I remember thinking how young, handsome, and inspiring he was. I personally felt hopeful. I believed and trusted in him. I heard and read that he was a man of God. A devoted Catholic. I also thought his wife, the first lady, was classy and beautiful.

In our living room, we had a small TV with a small screen. I do not know how we afforded one, but perhaps it was a gift from our father's mother, our beloved grandmother, Sara Ann. I believe it was an old Philco model, but I cannot trust my memory for sure. I just remember sitting cross-legged on the floor, scooted a short distance back from the tiny screen, and intently watching and listening to all of it. I have a faint but fond childhood memory of watching Soupy Sails, Shirley Temple movies, which were my personal favorites, and Howdy Doody. Also, the whole family enjoyed big-time laughs watching Wile E. Coyote and the Road Runner. A little later, as a teenager, American Band Stand became my favorite.

In Kennedy's first year in office, he was advised to build up our military, economic, and technical aid in South Vietnam to help with their defense and show greater power against the Viet Cong threat. At this time, the country was learning more and more about the growing tensions of the widely opposed Vietnam War. Another time of great tragedy, death, and destruction in our history and life.

In November 1963, the whole world was in shock. Kennedy was assassinated in Dallas, Texas. I was in school that day when I first heard the news. That day for sure is not a faint memory to me. It is a vivid memory of being in shock, disbelief, and heartbroken. Who and why I questioned, would want to kill our president? It was a very somber and sad day. A feeling of hopelessness surrounded many everywhere in all walks of life, at all ages. I questioned, *What kind of world do we live in?* In 1963, I was twelve years old.

What I was not aware of at that very same time was that my cousins were in much deeper despair and surrounded with fear and feelings of hopelessness. It was in this same year that their mother, Evelyn, was sent to the state penitentiary. They had lost their home, their father, their mother, and to make matters worse, the children were crying and holding on to each other as they were separated and abruptly hauled off and put into foster care with complete strangers who now had control of their lives.

CHAPTER SEVEN

MR. S. AND HIS KINDNESS

I have no real clear memory of my mother's father and stepmother, my grandparents ever being at our house when I was a kid. If they ever were, it might have been only once.

One particular year a few weeks before Christmas, our mother, Elizabeth handed me, my brother, and my sister a catalog mail-order book and told us we could pick out one item each as a gift for my mother's parents. She gave us a price range of about $2.00 to spend on them. I remember having and asking a million and one questions of my mom because we did not know our grandparents. I had no idea what they might like.

I wanted their gifts to be extra special because they were my grandparents. But more importantly, these were the grandparents we never saw and who never came to see us. Maybe they would love us if they liked our gift, I thought. Our handmade Christmas card that I had planned to make saying how much we loved them would also help.

My mother shared with us that they liked to bowl. The three of us kids sat down together, and we thoroughly went through the gift catalog. We finally decided and picked out matching bowling towels for them. They were cool, as I remember. They had a big picture of a bowling pin on them. So, it was not just a bowling towel. There was an additional cost to have their names put on. That cost would put us over budget, so we did not add their names. It was a big deal that we were able to purchase any gifts at all because there were several Christmas celebrations that there was not much at all under our tree. One thing we could always count on was that our grandmother Sara Ann and her mother, Rachel, our wonderful great-grandmother, would come with gifts to brighten the day and have lots of hugs and kisses as well.

This gift-giving brought to the surface and reminded my brother and sister, who then asked if our grandparents might have any presents for us. I had not thought about that. It did, however, dredge up the known fact and memory that we had not ever received a gift from them. More importantly, there was also no memory of any hugs either.

The Christmas holiday time and the meaning of Christmas at our church was such a beautiful time for myself and my siblings. Our church was within walking distance from our house, so growing up as kids, we were able to attend often. Our parents did not attend church regularly, but our mother attended for the Christmas holiday to see us perform in the Christmas pageant.

The Christmas Eve program at church was always special. The reenactment of the birth of Jesus, The Three Wisemen, Joseph, and Mary. Tryouts were exciting and started weeks before. To be chosen for any part made you feel special. The special meaning of Christmas seemed to always be a reset for me in my faith. A time when I prayed harder, had more faith, and had more hope.

I did not find out until after my mom had passed away that there was a period of over six years that my mom did not speak to her parents. Specifically, her dad. This information was shared with me by my cousins.

The story told is that one year my mom bought a TV for her dad and stepmother. This surprised me because I know money was very tight for almost all the years I lived at home. But I can see my mom doing without for herself to be able to give to them. The story is that my grandmother and grandfather did not like the TV she bought for them as a gift. Her dad called her and told her so. It hurt my mom and, at the same time, made her angry. Her dad told her to pick it up, he did not want it, and when she refused, he told her that he was setting it out at the road for the garbage men to haul it away to the dump. He did set it out at the street, and she did not speak to him because of this for the next six years.

Revealing and hearing this story helped to put a few things in place for me. It helped to provide a reason why we did not see our grandparents. At least for six of the years that they were absent from our lives.

It also brought to the surface the question of why I never asked my mom the reason we did not see her parents. What was it about me that I did not press her about this? I have no answer for this unless it could be that I was afraid of what the answer might be. I was afraid it might hurt more to know. The answer might have been because they do not love you.

Finding out about their not speaking for six years did help with the hurt I felt when I would see my grandfather in town. When I was walking to the grocery store and my grandfather would look away and not even say hello, or how are you. I did think the reason he acted that way was because he did not love me. That was hurtful and emotional for me. Feeling loved and wanted was already a struggle for me at home.

One day after being ignored by my grandfather as I was walking to the grocery store, when I arrived at the store, I remember the owner opening the wooden screen door for me and reaching in his pocket for his clean white handkerchief, and wiping away my tears and then pulling me in with a reassuring hug. He said whatever was wrong, God would make it right. It would all be better by the time I left his store.

The grocery store we shopped at was owned by a wonderful grocer named Mr. S. He knew our family was poor and that buying candy was not an option that was allowed in our house. However, every time I shopped, he had a special coupon or a special deal that would take money off, and I could choose some candy to take home. My brother and sister were always anxiously waiting at the door when I got home to see what great deal I was able to make. I was many years older before I realized that all this bartering at his store was his gift to us. There was no special coupon. He was truly a wonderful person. I remember seeing him and his family volunteering often at another church in our community. I remember hearing from others in the neighborhood as I grew older what a wonderful and giving man he was.

He left a warm, positive childhood memory for me.

Dear Lord, I am truly thankful for Mr. S. and his kindness.

CHAPTER EIGHT

FOSTER CARE

Immediately following Evelyn's sentencing to the state penitentiary, Katie, the oldest, at age ten, and her two younger sisters, Maria, aged six, and Cynthia, aged five, were being escorted out of the courthouse to a foster care home. While Nancy, age nine, and Max, age seven, were taken to another foster home.

Screaming, crying, trying to hold onto each other, they were tugged apart and abruptly hauled off in separate vehicles.

For Katie, upon arriving at the foster home, the welcome-to-our-home feeling never happened. The foster parents had three of their own children. They had a daughter that was the same age as Katie and two younger boys.

Immediately, the daughter decided she did not like Katie, and she made it her goal to make it known to her that she was in charge. She went out of her way to do bad things like painting fingernail polish all over the wood of the bed she slept in and then blaming Katie. Making messes in the kitchen and blaming her, destroying things in the house, and even hiding things from her parents and then blaming Katie. It was clear this foster home daughter would stop at nothing to get her in trouble, to get her out of their house.

The parents were extremely strict with Katie, Maria, and Cynthia but not with their own children, even though Maria and Cynthia were very young at the time.

Katie, Maria, and Cynthia were also not allowed to see each other. The foster parents went to great lengths to keep them separated from each other, including not letting them even eat together. Bedtime was terribly frightening for them, trying to understand all the extreme measures and methods they went to in separating them from each other. They put up barricades between the beds so that they could not see each other. The parents put boxes and crates stacked up high against their beds to block them off from each other's view. They were also forbidden to even dare move any of the boxes.

To this day, it has been hard to understand why these people felt it was so important to keep them from seeing each other, talking to each other, eating together. One would think that the reason for putting them in the same home in the first place was to keep at least three of the kids together because they were from the same family. Their own children were not separated from each other. They ate together, played together. Answers and reasons for this treatment remain unknown. But it was hurtful, and it broke their little hearts.

Katie was not at this foster home for long. In fact, it might have been less than two weeks before she heard a knock on the door and a stranger's voice, and the next thing, she knew she was ordered to march up the stairs to the bedroom and collect her things; she was moving out. She was not allowed to tell her sisters goodbye. They had been put in another room with closed doors so they would not be able to see or know what was happening. And no one at the house said goodbye or shared with her what was happening next. She was told to get in the car and to not ask any questions.

Maria and Cynthia suffered some incredibly sad days at this house. It did not qualify as a home, maybe a prison. The punishment that they both vividly remember is the days and nights they spent in the dark on a stairway. The stairway had a door at the top and a door at the bottom. Both girls spent large amounts of time locked between those two doors, one girl at the top and one at the bottom. They were not allowed to speak to each other while locked in the dark on the stairs. Sometimes they spent an entire day there with nothing to eat, no bathroom breaks, and many nights, they also had to sleep there. Such a harsh and cruel punishment given for dropping a spoon on the floor while eating, spilling a glass of milk by accident, or dropping a crumb on the floor.

The daughter had long fingernails, and she took great pleasure in scratching Maria and Cynthia. She would pinch hard and scratch their face, arms, back, legs; it did not matter. She would punch them too. Sadly, she could do it, and she was never punished for it.

Cynthia would sometimes have an accident at night and wet the bed. When the foster mother discovered this in the morning, it would result in both girls being whipped and put on the stairs for the entire day. One day Maria heard Cynthia crying from her bed on the other side of the boxes and crates, and she asked her what was wrong. She said she had an accident and wet the bed. Maria pushed her way through the crates and got in bed with her to hold her. When the foster mother came into the room and saw them in bed together, Maria took the blame for Cynthia and said she had been the one to wet the bed. They both were still whipped and put on the stairs for the day for punishment.

Maria started to have a strong feeling that she really needed to try harder every day to protect her little sister. She could at least try to help because it made her sad when her little sister cried.

Katie had been taken to a new house that she referred to as being like a ranch. The foster parents had an older son about two or three years older than Katie, who was mean and had a bad temper. This was not a good foster family either.

At the ranch, they had horses, sheep, and a big barn. She was expected to bail hay, which she had never done before, and lots of other chores. Outside chores and inside the house chores. She attended the same school as the son of this family. She did not have any friends, and no one tried or wanted to be friends with her at school. She was labeled as being different because she was in foster care. Other parents frowned on their children associating with her.

One day after school, Katie asked permission to go with their son to the park. She had no friends of her own, so even though he was mean to her, she still wanted to go. At the park, they met up with a group of other boys. On the way home, Katie and the boys stopped at a nearby garage. They all went inside, and the next thing that happened is the boys started groping her and touching her in different places. Katie described this as having their way with her. She was hurt, shocked, and scared. When she returned to the foster home, she told the foster mother what had happened. It was that same night a car came, then a knock on the door, and she was sent once again to her bedroom to pack up her few things and leave this house too.

The next house for Katie was the house where her sister Nancy was.

Nancy and Max had originally been together at a big farmhouse since the day they were taken from the courthouse. These foster parents were extremely mean. The father was not as mean as his wife. She seemed to especially enjoy the beatings she gave. She had a medium build and may have been around the age of thirty. The father seemed to work a lot, so the foster mother was in charge. For Max at age seven, living at this house was a much worse experience for him than his sister Nancy. One day, he forgot to take his dirty dishes from the table to the kitchen sink after lunch. For this, he was beaten first with a long whip and then a belt, and he was then locked in a round building that was way out behind the house. He was left there in the dark, no supper and nothing to drink, and he had to sleep on the floor, locked in the dark for the night. After she beat him and locked him up, she said, "I'll teach you boy so that you never forget again."

At seven years old, he had lots of chores that he had to do. The foster mother made it her passion to punish him with beatings until she had no energy left in her and then lock him up for the night. One day in school, after a night of beatings, he was not able to sit in his chair at school. When he was asked what was wrong, he told the teacher that his foster mother beat him so bad he could not sit down. The teacher called the social worker's office, and they came to the house that afternoon to talk to the foster parents. Max had no idea that anyone had called or that they were coming to the house. When the social worker asked him about how he was treated, he told her the truth. That night he had another beating from the foster mother for telling. What the foster mother did not expect is the social worker made a surprise visit the very next day. What the social worker saw on little Max were fresh new bruises and welts from another beating. That night both Max and his sister Nancy were taken from that foster home.

Max, thinking back on this experience years later, said that all the thoughts of her were like living in hell with an evil and wicked stepmother.

For Nancy, her memories are many nights and more nights than she wants to remember, of her little brother being locked in a dark building, without food and water, after he had been beaten to a pulp. She would cry herself to sleep.

Nancy cried out, "Please send someone to save us." "Someone, please hear us crying; please come to help us."

Next, Max went to a small group home, and shortly after that he was taken to another foster home on a farm. There were two boys living there with their parents. They were twins about four years old. When the foster parents went to the store, they left Max in charge, and he was only seven years old. If the twin boys would accidentally make a mess or get hurt, Max was in trouble. The foster mother yelled all the time, but she never hit him. But the foster father took enjoyment in teaching Max lessons and beat him often with switches and his belt. His room better be clean; there were no warnings and no second chances. For Max and the foster care homes, he just kept moving from one nightmare to the next.

The abuse was so bad for him that he would rock in his bed at night. This would cause further whippings and beatings for him because he was not lying down, being quiet, and sleeping. He could not help the rocking, and so he suffered many beatings because of it.

The next home that Nancy was sent to, and Katie joined her there too sometime later, was the only good foster home the children had. Only two out of the five children were able to experience something good in foster care. At this foster home, the mother was pregnant with her first child. Nancy remembers her having a nice smile, being very petite, and extremely sweet and caring. She always wore her hair in a ponytail. Both girls loved living there and thought that the foster father was wonderful too.

The girls rode bikes; they could play and were allowed to be kids and have fun. The chores were easy. Washing dishes, setting the table. No punishments. Lots of hugs, and the girls loved their foster parents.

This was the only home that celebrated holidays like Christmas that included Katie and Nancy. For the other children, none of them ever had a birthday celebration while in foster care, and there were no presents for any of them for Christmas.

This time in all their lives is hard to understand and make any sense of. The children were taken away from their mother. She was handcuffed and hauled off to the state penitentiary because she left them at home alone at times to walk directly across the street to clean motel rooms and serve as a night clerk. This job she had was to put food on the table for her children and provide them with shelter. What our legal and court system did was to call her unfit to be a mother, that she was endangering them. She could not afford a babysitter. She was doing what she felt was best for her children.

The legal system at that time placed Elizabeth's children in the hands of social workers and foster homes, where they suffered severe beatings, torture, neglect, and a lifetime of nightmares from the trauma. The system was acting in the capacity of being in the best interest of the children and what the children received were scars for a lifetime.

My cousins shared that what they have found is that the foster care system still has many issues today. A large percentage of abuse in the foster care system still exists. They believe that some, not all become foster parents more for the money than wanting to provide good care and protection for a child. Social workers are underpaid and short-staffed. Most children are afraid to speak up because of being threatened and then suffering a worst beating for coming forward. Or being afraid the next home they could be sent to might be even worse.

One must wonder what their life might have looked like and turned out if their mother had not been turned in to the authorities. If only she would have been able to stay working across the street at the motel and providing for her kids. But that tragically is not the path their lives took, and this was a very painful time for them.

Evelyn legally divorced her husband while in prison in 1962. They had been married for ten years.

Evelyn was released from prison exactly one year after being put behind bars. She and the children never saw each other while she was in prison. For the younger children, their mother just disappeared from their memory.

Her eighteen-month sentence was reduced after going in front of the parole board, and she was released on probation and with some strict requirements that she had to meet before she might even possibly re-gain custody of her children. Those requirements were; first, she had to be what the child services board considered stable, have a good job, and a clean home that was large enough to house five children.

Sometime after Evelyn's release, she was able to set up

a visit with her children at the foster homes they were each housed at. The youngest daughters, Maria and Cynthia, did not remember her at all and did not understand how she could be their mother. For that day, the foster parents dressed Maria and Cynthia all up like it was Easter and in frilly Easter dresses. The foster parents gave the impression that everything was good for the kids and that they were well taken care of.

For Max, his mother's visit gave him hope, and he was incredibly happy to see her. He was happy to know that sometime soon, his life and the hell he was living would be over. His mother was finally coming to rescue him. The days forward for him were easier to bear. Knowing and waiting for his mother to come back for him helped to get him through the days that followed.

For Katie, she said her mother did not visit her during her time and stay in foster care. She never questioned why, and she did not take it to heart either. She thought it to be just something that did not work out for her. Nancy had no memory of her mother coming for a visit and since she was happy with the home that she was in she did not feel slight-ed, nor did she care. If her mother would have come to visit and the truth would have been told, she would have told her mother that she wanted to stay with the foster family. She loved them, she was happy, they were good to her. They were her family now.

My cousins did not understand why all of this was happening to them, but each of them never stopped hoping for something better.

"When you pass through the waters, I will be with you, and when you pass through the rivers, they will not sweep over you. When you walk through the fire, you will not be burned; the flames will not set you ablaze" (Isaiah, 43:2).

CHAPTER NINE

SHE WORE A BLUE SUIT ON HER WEDDING DAY

The year was 1964, when Evelyn was released from prison. After a short while, she was able to find a job at a diner as a waitress in the small Ohio town where she grew up. It had been about two years since she lost custody of her children. At this same time, her sister Elizabeth was still living in the same small town with her husband and three children.

On April 13, 1965, on Palm Sunday, a deadly tornado struck six states, including Iowa, Illinois, Indiana, Ohio, Michigan, and Wisconsin. The tornado that struck Ohio hit awfully close to the small town where they all lived. This caused damage that stretched across the close and nearby neighboring areas. It was an F-4 tornado, and it was reported to be the second deadliest in Ohio history. One specific newspaper picture that was terrifying was of a bus that was traveling with passengers on the interstate. The bus was lifted in the air and then flipped over until dropping up-side-down on the road. It crushed the top of the bus all the way down to past the windows of the bus, and five of the passengers were killed.

It was sad and terrifying. A tornado with this force had never hit our area before. A tornado touching down that caused so much death and destruction. There were many prayers thanking God for sparing lives and more prayers for all the others who were less fortunate.

The highlight of 1965 for myself and being a fourteen-year-old teenager was being in love with the Beatles. Especially Paul. My father's mother Sara Ann and great-grand-mother Becky lived together on a farm. My grandmother's younger brother lived next door with his family. Whenever I went to stay at my grandmother's house, my girl cousins who lived next door also loved the Beatles, and they always wanted to hang out. It was Beatle mania the whole time I stayed there. We would argue over who could have which of the Beatle's band members as our boyfriend. As though that was even a possibility. What a stupid thing to argue about. What big imaginations we all had.

Of course, their mother, my aunt Giselle, who I adored, had a crush on Elvis Presley, and whenever I went inside the house, she had the phonograph playing with all her

Elvis' favorites. "Blue Suede Shoes" and "Hunka, Hunka" comes to mind. She could swing her hips to all his songs and belt out the words because she knew them all. She was really a cool aunt.

I remember one day I was outside, and my aunt called me to come inside; she wanted to talk to me. One of my cousins said to me that I was in big trouble now. I went in to see my aunt while trying to have an innocent look on my face, and I stood quietly and innocently in front of her waiting for the big trouble that was about to come down on me. My aunt Giselle said that her daughter Darlene had come into the house crying because I had told her that the outfit that she was wearing looked like she was wearing pajamas. My aunt explained to me that her outfit was not pajamas, and I had hurt my cousin Darlene's feelings. I remember I did not hesitate for a minute, and I politely said to my aunt, "Well, I could tell Darlene a lie and say that her outfit looked nice, and then God would be upset with me because her outfit does look like pajamas, or I could tell her the truth, and then you could be mad at me. I would rather you be mad at me because you would just threaten me with the wooden spoon. But aunt Gisele, God keeps track of all these kinds of things, and I want him to be happy with me. I don't want to lie." I remember she laughed; she hugged me and asked me to please be nicer to Darlene because Darlene was extremely sensitive. Many years later, before my aunt passed away, she asked me to promise her that I would watch over Darlene when she was gone. She said Darlene always loved me the most of all her cousins, and aunt Gisele knew I would watch out for her. I was a tough guy.

Spending time on the farm with both of my grandmothers and my cousins next door on my dad's side are some of my fondest memories growing up. When my cousins and I were a few years younger, my great grandmother would pack a lunch for us girls, and we would walk down to the culvert tile in the ditch at the corner and just hang out there for the day. We were not aware at the time of possible leaches or that this might even be a weird place for girls to hang out. I do remember garter snakes, but that was not a big scare either. For us, it was like our fort. Our secret hideaway. We did a lot of play-acting there. We got excited when we could hear a car passing by or a farm tractor. The drivers had no idea we were in the culvert hanging out. We would giggle after they passed over.

At my cousins' house in the backyard, next door to my grandma's, there was a giant weeping willow tree. God, it was majestic. I remember spending lots of time laying on the bare ground underneath it and looking through the branches and up at the sky. The clouds and the shapes of the clouds fascinated me. I dreamed about life and what it would be like when I was all grown up. I thought of endless possibilities lying under that tree. I always felt safe there, and I would dream about lots of different things. I dreamed about being a good parent and how much I would love my children. Laying there and looking up at the sky, I felt closer to heaven and God. I believed that the angels were there just beyond the clouds, and sometimes I thought I saw the shape of angels and their faces in the clouds, and I would talk to them.

Years later, in life, my husband and I bought a house in the country with a large weeping willow tree. The tree was one of the most favorite things I liked about that house. It was always a calming reminder of past days enjoying the breeze, the clouds, the calmness, and the angels watching over me that had always comforted me as a child. The happier times in my childhood when I stayed at my grandma's.

It is 1965, and the skirts are getting shorter, and for the guys, their hair is getting longer. I am really starting to think more about boys. I want to try and be prettier. I want to fit in. I want to be popular, but I don't know how.

In this same year, the Vietnam war was continuing to worsen, and the life casualties kept growing for military and civilians. I am hearing about some older boys in our town that were drafted and boys from the area around us that are fighting in this war. I remember hearing about the injuries and deaths of some of our boys. On November 13 of that year, the Anti-War movement protestors staged a large march on Washington to protest the war. I was glued to the news to learn more about this. This was life outside of my little town. This is what is going on in our country and our world. I am praying more. I am more aware of life. I am growing up.

I had no idea my mother's sister Evelyn had been in prison and that her children had been in foster care for almost two years. I did not know that her kids were being abused and suffering. I did not know that they felt alone and abandoned and not loved.

I do not think my mom knew either about their time and life while they were in foster care. It was never discussed with me then or even years later. If I had known, I would have been praying for them. I would have hoped that if I had known, I could have been a voice for them from the outside. They desperately needed somebody, and nobody was there. Nobody showed up to help them. I learned the truth about this more than fifty years later. I am shocked, sad, and heartbroken for what they had to live through.

I do have a vague memory of hearing my mom talk about my aunt Evelyn getting remarried in late 1965. Her new husband's name was Heban. He was a truck driver that she met while working at the diner, and my mom said she was incredibly happy.

Evelyn wore a beautiful blue suit for her wedding day.

Evelyn's wedding day plan was that she and Heban would pick up her five children from foster care immediately after their wedding. They would load all her children in the car and swiftly take them to their brand-new home in the country. Their new home was a big, rented farmhouse that had big apple and peach trees in the yard. This special farm was within just a few miles of where my mom, dad, brother, sister, and I lived.

I never saw my cousins while they lived there. I never knew they did live there. I never saw my aunt or her new husband. I never heard about their life on that farm with the big apple trees and big peach trees until fifty-six years later.

CHAPTER TEN
THE WEDDING DAY

It was a warm and sunny day on July 31, 1965, when Evelyn married Heban Harris on the steps of the courthouse in Ohio. The courthouse was just a few miles outside of the little town where she grew up. Heban was a tall man with dark hair and dark eyes. He was a truck driver, and he had been coming into the small-town diner where Evelyn worked. He started coming in more and more often, and it was just to see Evelyn. He had set his sights on this beautiful young woman with long dark curly hair, big beautiful eyes, and a great smile.

The full details of their courtship are not known by her children. Details like, how long had they dated? What attracted their mother to him? How did he treat her then? Did her sister or parents meet him and like him?

What seemed to be the most likely reason that Evelyn chose to marry him was that Heban's proposal included him promising to help her get her kids back. Heban had told her they would make a home for all her children. He made the promise to her that they were going to become one big happy family. What was most important to Evelyn was gaining back full custody of her children. Every day since the day she was released from prison, she had been working towards that goal. She was doing all that she could to meet the requirements made of her to gain her children back. This new hero of a man in her life was a dream come true. Her knight in shining armor. He was willing to take on five children for her. He must love her dearly, she thought. How many men would agree to take on five young children and feed and clothe them? Especially because he was not their natural father and he had never even met them. Their own natural father had not stepped up to do that, so Heban's proposal was a huge commitment.

To her, Heban was like the perfect man. Her new hero had come to save the day. At this moment in time, Evelyn felt like she was a fairy princess living out her life in an incredibly special fairytale. Her prince had arrived. Evelyn was thirty years old.

Evelyn wore a new blue suit for her wedding day, and she looked beautiful. She was filled with excitement for this special day. The plan for the day had been discussed repeatedly. Immediately after saying their vows and being pronounced man and wife, they would drive to each of the foster homes where her children were living and pick them up. She would be swooping in and making a grand entrance because she wanted it to be a great big, beautiful Kodak moment. Their mother, along with her brand-new husband, was coming to pick up her kids and to save the day. She played the movie of what this would be like over and over in her head. Each time the movie reel played, it got better, happier, and more perfect. On this special day, she would regain custody of her five children, and the added bonus was they would have a new daddy too.

By this time, Evelyn had been apart from her children for over two years. This marriage to Heban would mean she had fulfilled the court's order to provide proof of stability, having financial resources, and providing suitable shelter. Heban and Evelyn had rented a large farmhouse in the country large enough for the whole family. She was thrilled with the thought of seeing her children's reaction on their faces when they surprised them with a big new farmhouse to live in. She pictured their happy and smiling faces. They would have their mother back, a new dad, and a new home. She had thought about this day coming for an awfully long time. It was all she focused on after that day in court when she received her sentence, and the children were taken away to foster care. She prayed and waited for this day.

When the foster parents were contacted about Evelyn gaining back custody, she had requested of the foster parents to please keep it a secret from her children. She explained that she wanted to surprise them. On that special day in July, the children were completely unaware that their mother was coming for them. That day had started out for them just like any other day.

Katie, the oldest child, did not remember the order in which the children were picked up first. She has a slight memory of seeing shadows of other kids in the car, but she does not remember any of the faces of who they might have been. What she does remember, and vividly, was seeing her mother right away because her mother had her car window rolled down and was waving out the window. Katie ran to the car crying and stumbling because she ran so fast. She hugged and kissed her mom and was filled with so much happiness, joy, and excitement. Katie said it felt like she was going to burst. Her heart was thumping right out of her chest. Next, Katie noticed that there was a man in the car. Someone she had never seen before. She asked, "Mommy, who is this man?" Her mom answered her and said, "His name is Heban, honey, and we got married today, and he is your new daddy."

Katie said that what it felt like for her at that moment was like having a wonderful dream come true for her. She was absolutely overjoyed. She had her mom back, and on top of it, she also had a new dad. She felt relief and a sense of peace. It would be good to erase all the past painful memories. It would be okay to have hope and look forward to a new life with her mom and new dad and to be finally joined together again with her brother and sisters. As the oldest child, she had always watched over her siblings. She had missed them so much. She had worried about them. Katie was twelve years old.

Max was overwhelmed with happiness to see his mom in the car smiling at him and to see her hanging out of the car window waving. She had finally come for him. She had promised him, and here she was. All this time, he wanted to believe she would be coming, but part of him was afraid to believe it. But by golly, he thought, here she is. He was overwhelmed with relief. Instantly, he turned his thoughts to trusting and believing that this would mean the horrible hell he had been living the last couple of years in foster care would finally be over. He was only six years old when he went into foster care, and now, he was eight. It felt like an eternity to him. There were many days he just wanted to give up. He felt hopeless. Of Evelyn's five children, it was poor Max that suffered the worst and the most abuse while in foster care. The kids had all compared notes when they were joined back together. The stories made them cry, but they cried the most for Max.

As Max and his mom made their way to the car, he remembers seeing one of his sisters already in the car. He is just not sure which one but thought it might have been Nancy. He also saw a man behind the steering wheel, and so he asked his mom who that was. His mom explained, "Honey, this is your new daddy." Max did not understand how you could just go and get yourself a new daddy and how that all worked, and so for the time being, he had decided he would just go along with it. After all, the most important thing was, he was back with his mommy.

Maria had a memory of her mom and the blue suit, but she did not remember having any emotion about her being there to pick her up. No feelings of excitement. Also, for that day, she did not remember that she even had other siblings, a brother, and two other sisters. She was only five years old when her mother was taken away, and she was separated from her siblings. What she was most excited about on that day was finding out that she did have a brother and two more big sisters. She felt she would have to learn a whole lot more to be able to understand the mom thing and what having a mom meant. It was different from the life she knew in foster care.

Cynthia was so little at age three when her mother was taken away she did not even remember she had a mother. With her mom picking her up at age five, she was really confused, but she remembers being happy anyways because everybody else was. The feeling was contagious. They were all smiling and happy, so she was too. Her big sister Maria held on tightly to her hand.

Nancy does not remember being or feeling excited at all to see her mother. The only thing she remembers is crying because she was sad. She truly did not want to leave where she was living to be with her mother and this new dad. She was completely happy staying right where she was. She liked living with her loving foster care parents. That was her home. Her stability. She deeply loved her foster parents and her life there, and she really did not want to be forced to leave. But it was explained to her that she did not get a choice. She had to go. Her memory is one of being unhappy about this news and that this was an incredibly sad day for her. She was nine.

After Evelyn and Heban had picked up all the children,

they headed directly to the big two-story farmhouse in the country. Pulling into the driveway, Katie said that her first reaction was, "Wow—we are now officially in paradise."

Heban and their mother allowed the children to get out of the car and run up the steps, throw open the wooden screen door, and run inside the house. They ran through the house from room to room to check it out and see the layout. Next, they ran up the stairs to pick out their bedrooms. It was so unbelievably exciting. It almost seemed too good to be true after living the way they all had while in foster care for the past two years. That is except for Nancy, who had loved her foster home.

For each of them, looking back and remembering and reflecting on the first few weeks living at the farmhouse and the time they all spent together as a new family, all five of them remember this time as being great. It was a new beginning and happy memories. The family all had their meals together; they played board games together and told stories. The children all had chores but nothing hard. Typical chores like washing dishes, making your bed, and keeping your room clean. Katie said it was like a regular episode right out of Ozzie and Harriett's family life. It was wonderful. Truly a dream come true.

CHAPTER ELEVEN

THE FARMHOUSE

After Living at the farmhouse for a few weeks and getting adjusted to each other, Heban started taking on a different attitude of how things were now going to be around there. He started using a harsh mean voice when he spoke to the children, and he made it known very quickly and clearly that he was the man of the house, their daddy, and therefore their boss. That he was the one and the only one in charge over everything, their living breathing daily lives and not their mom. Each day that passed, the true meaning of what this meant became more and more frighteningly clear. He became more demanding, yelling, pushing, throwing things at them, smacking, slugging them in the back of their head, beatings with belts, whips, rubber hoses, and more. He would assign them with impossible demands and chores, knowing full well they would fail because they were doomed before they started. Impossible, unrealistic, and timed demands.

The assignments were not meant to be fair. Upon not being able to meet his demands and within the allotted time that he had given, it was their own fault. Heban would tell them that they had brought this unfortunate situation and punishment on themselves. That they needed to be taught a lesson. He would beat them for this, and then they would have to start all over with the same assignment with the warning that this next time they had better try harder to get it right, or it would happen all over again. There was never room for discussion. It meant that as sure as the sun sets every night that you were going to get a beating. You were a worthless human being who failed at everything you were told to do. You could not do anything right, so you had brought this punishment on yourself. Five young, terrified stepchildren learned very quickly exactly what all this meant for them. Their days and nights grew darker and left them without any hope. Each of them felt the same way. What possibly could there be to look forward to in their lives. Each of them asked themselves and each other, "Is this what life is like for all kids?" Heban, their new daddy, had told them it was.

In the evening, after the supper dishes were done and the family was gathered in the living room, Heban started motioning for Katie to come over and sit on her daddy's lap, and he would rub her back while she was sitting there. She compared this time to feel special and appreciated as the oldest child. Her mother was working the evening shift at the diner, so Katie had been trying to help more. Katie was trying to help keep things calmer. Trying to find a way to please Heban and make him happy to help stop the beatings on all of them. Katie felt that Heban must have been noticing how hard she was working around the house, and this special attention he was giving to her was his way of showing her some fatherly love and his extra appreciation of her.

One night when their mom was at work, Heban told Katie to go upstairs and clean her room. He told the other kids to stay downstairs and to behave themselves. Heban followed Katie upstairs to her bedroom and shut the door behind them. She felt for sure she was in big trouble now, and she was wondering what she had done wrong. She asked him if everything was okay and if she was doing a good job. He told her she was doing a good job and to sit down on the bed; he wanted to talk with her. He patted her on the shoulder as reassurance that this was just a father-daughter conversation. As they sat together on the bed, he started rubbing her in different places. At this age, she did not really know about sex, so she was not sure about what was happening to her. While she was in foster care, the events that took place with the boys in the garage were the boys holding her down, feeling, touching, and rubbing on her. They had not raped her. She was still a virgin.

Katie, being confused and frightened by what was happening, wanted to scream out for help. The next thing that happened was Heban pushing her down hard on the bed, and then he climbed on top of her. Katie begged and begged him to please get off her. He was so heavy, and it was hard for her to breathe. Katie started panicking, and Heban became angry because she was struggling with him, and he started slapping her and holding her down, and then he raped her. Katie cried and begged him to please get off; "Please, stop. It hurts. I cannot breathe." When he was finished and finally rolled off her little young body, he leaned over her and said, "You need to stop crying. Everything will be all right. This is what you do in life. You are exactly the right age to learn this." Then he added, "And don't tell your mother." He threatened her and repeated it to her again "Do not tell your mother. If you do, you will get a beating, and then you will go to the orphanage, and your mother will go back to jail." He reassured her again that all of this was completely normal and a part of life and said, "This is how it is for all girls."

For Katie, from that day on, everything at the farmhouse changed. The physical abuse became worse, and Heban was having his way with her whenever he wanted.

Katie kept remembering what her new dad, Heban, had said to her that day, "This is what you do in life." She kept thinking, *So this is how life is for all girls?* It was hard for her to believe and think that this horrible nightmare of a life that she was living was what her life was going to look like now and forever. Worry filled her mind, not for just herself but also for her siblings and her mother.

She began to think about the other kids in school and their fathers. She wondered about other families. Is it a father's role to beat and molest you? To yell at you, throws things at you, slug you. To give you endless chores and then yell at you that you are stupid and you never do anything right. To tell you that you are worthless.

Katie was so distraught she felt sick to her stomach most of the time. She was constantly on edge and terribly frightened, not knowing whether when she took her very next breath if she would be beaten, raped, or both. She never felt safe after that. She was even fearful of going to sleep at night. She grew more tired and carried very deep hopelessness and sadness inside of her and outwardly on her face. Her smile was completely gone.

Katie remembers that eventually and much later, her

mother, Evelyn, figured out what had been going on. Whenever her mother would try to stop Heban, he would throw Evelyn hard to the ground and start beating on her until she was bloody, and sometimes, he would beat her close to unconsciousness. He made it perfectly clear to Evelyn and her children that this was his house, he was the boss, their boss, and they all had to do exactly as he said. Evelyn and her children were utterly terrified of him. Heban constantly threatened Evelyn with the threat she feared the most. He reminded her if she tried leaving or telling anyone, he would make sure she would be going back to prison for the rest of her life, and her kids would be going to an orphanage.

Shortly after they all moved to the farmhouse, Heban's parents came to live with them. One would hope another set of eyes and ears in the house might stop the madness, but instead, it intensified it. Heban's father was a drunk, and his mother, in the beginning, started out nice. But sadly, that did not last long. She turned out to be a very hateful and nasty person.

The kids called Heban's mother Mamaw because that is what she wanted to be called. Heban's mother and family grew up in the hills of Kentucky, and that was a typical endearing granny, grandma name. Mamaw took great joy in tattling on the children and embellishing the story to make matters worse for them whenever she could. She also did not like Evelyn at all, and so she made every effort to tell her about all her shortcomings. She would get right up in Evelyn's face and tell her she was stupid and ugly. She also made up and embellished stories about things that Evelyn did to get her into trouble with her son, Heban.

Heban's father was called Papaw. He was a terrible drunk and would sometimes leave the house and be gone so long that Heban would go out searching for him. It was not unusual to find him passed out in a ditch or along the side of the road. Heban would drag him back to the house and beat him to a pulp all the while his dad would be yelling and swearing at him. Heban did not spare his temper with his mother either. On plenty of occasions, Nancy talked about seeing her being slapped and knocked to the ground by her own son.

Maria talked about Heban's daughter from his first marriage. She had come to live with them for a short time, but she had kind of a breakdown and had to be hospitalized. Maria remembered feeling sad for her. The children later found out she had been abused by her own father too.

For Cynthia, arriving at the farmhouse or having any

memories of her time living there are all absent. All that she can remember is this house had a stairway with a door at the bottom and a door at the top. The foster care house she lived in also had a door at the top and one at the bottom. This was so vivid in her memory because she lived a lot of her young life between two doors. Sitting on the steps between two doors with her sister Maria at the bottom and her at the top was her everyday life while she was in foster care. She thought that this is how you lived. She grew up thinking for a long time that all houses were built this way, and this is where kids lived and spent their days.

Nancy, at nine years old, not quite ten yet, had many haunting memories about living at the farmhouse, starting with the wooden screen door to the house. The door served as a reminder that once you opened that door and walked inside, you were at constant risk. For Nancy, the farmhouse is when her life in hell began.

The memories of suffering through what seemed to be never-ending hopelessness. There were no happy sunshine days, just days of darkness, sadness, and more abuse. Nancy also remembered and shared that Heban's daughter had a break down from the abuse that she had suffered by her dad when he lived and was married to his first wife.

THE FARMHOUSE

One day, Nancy decided to shave her legs even though she had been told she had to wait until she was age twelve. Her older sister Katie was shaving, and her legs looked so smooth and pretty. Nancy decided she could probably sneak and do it, so she went upstairs to the bathroom to do just that. Nancy cut her legs so badly that there was blood everywhere. The cuts on her legs could not be hidden. Fear overwhelmed her about the trouble she would be in. When her mom and Heban found out, much to her surprise, she did not suffer a beating because she was already in such bad shape. Her punishment was that she was forbidden to shave again until age sixteen as her punishment. That would be six more years.

One of Heban's favorite mean things to do was to tromp up the stairs to the girl's bedroom they shared and begin tearing everything apart. He would completely strip the neatly made beds, take all their clothes out of the closet, the dressers, shoes, and anything else he could find of theirs in the room to throw into a heap on the floor. He would then demand that all four girls come up to their room and clean their mess, and this time, they had better do it right. Sometimes this went on all night long without sleep, and then they had to go to school the next morning. Tired, beaten, and told over and over how stupid and worthless they all were.

Soon Heban started telling Nancy to come to lay down with daddy in his and her mother's downstairs bedroom. This would happen when Evelyn was at work at the diner. The sexual abuse had started for her too. She was not quite ten years old. Heban also threatened her like he had Katie. She was not to say a word to her mother or any of her siblings, and if she did, he would beat her, her mother would go back to prison, and all the kids would be taken to the orphanage.

Nancy would look out the screen door to the outside yard and think about how much fun it would be to go outside. She wanted to climb the fruit trees and run around the big yard, but you needed permission to be able to go outside. Asking to go outside was a simple ask for most children but for Nancy in her house, it came with a cost. Nancy had to spend special time in the bedroom with Heban first, and then she would be allowed to play outside. Whenever Heban wanted and when no one else was close by, he would slip his hands in her pants. For Nancy, it felt like she was his personal property, and she had to keep Heban happy. That was her daughterly duty. Going with Heban on car rides to the pharmacy or store has left her with unbelievably bad memories. Nancy endured it all and yet kept silent. She was terrified of the consequences, the threat of going to the orphanage and her mother going back to prison. She worried for her mother because she had seen her beat so many times before. Heban would push her to the ground and beat her until she was bloody. Sometimes Nancy feared that her mother might not get back up because she was dead. Nancy knew full well her mother could not protect her from Heban. Her mother could not even protect herself. Heban was just too strong, too powerful, too dangerous to be able to fight off.

There were never any real conversations allowed at the house. Everything was sugar-coated, and the rule was you were only allowed to speak when you were spoken to. If there was anything good about living at that house, it was overshadowed by all the abuse. It was a constant struggle trying to understand the difference between love and hate. This could not possibly be called love.

Nancy tried digging deep into her memories for anything good in this life. Besides climbing the fruit trees, there were days of picking dandelions and hooking the stems together to make a necklace, playing ring around the rosy with her siblings. Singing. A few happy memories that always quickly faded. They were always overshadowed and drowned out by the flood of terrifying and evil memories that came rushing in.

Nancy's abuse started at the young age of nine and con-tinued daily, sometimes twice a day, until she left home for good. Her everyday life was filled with constant fear. To this day, she suffers from stomach issues and has trouble eating without becoming sick. Sometimes she is in bed for days.

Max tried to remember about life at the farmhouse, but all his memories he has blocked out. He cannot remember anything after the first few days of being there. Max said, "After we first moved to the farmhouse, it sure seemed like we were all one big happy family, but then the rest and all the days after are all erased from my mind."

It was about a year later that Evelyn told the kids the whole family was moving to Indiana. Max asked what In-diana was, not knowing it was a state. His mom explained where it was and how far and what a beautiful place they would have. She described a big pond behind the house where you can swim and fish. "It was going to be like par-adise," she told him. Max said his mom then told him to go to his bedroom and pack up his things. He grabbed a big cardboard box, and he stuffed anything and everything in it. Max was ready to go. He was going fishing.

PRELUDE TO MOVING TO INDIANA

Each told their story separately and apart from each other. The recollections of what took place for all of them were the same. Not one of them told a different story about what had happened in their lives. Each of them was able to confirm what they had suffered.

Any holding out for hope that the abuse might not have been as bad as you thought proved to be false hope.

They had all somehow, by the grace of God, lived through it. They had all struck a pact and a bond to stick together to survive. They saw it, they heard it, and they lived it every day.

CHAPTER TWELVE

MOVING TO INDIANA: NANCY

All the kids were piled in the car with Heban and their mother. Driving down the highway, Nancy could see from the car wind  in the back seat the big green house her mo was pointing to and excitedly saying, "Look kids, look, that is our new house right there." The kids wiggled around in the car to get a good look. Surrounding the house was a huge parking lot with other businesses on it. It was quite a spread and a lot for all of them to see and take in. Her mom went on to say with great enthusiasm and excitement, "Look, that there is our motel, our restaurant, and our gas station too. All of that is ours. We own all of it," she said proudly.

Heban and Evelyn had some financial help from Heban's parents, who had sold their home even before they all had moved into the farmhouse. The property they bought included a big house that was painted green, a motel, a gas/service station, and a restaurant on a large parcel of land.

There were big blinking signs on the property for all highway travelers to easily see that on this exit, there was a motel, a restaurant, and gas. Behind the house was a big pond that the kids had been told that they could go swimming and fishing in. This dream come true adventure they were being told about was now right outside the car window. It was real, it was right in front of them at the next exit, and it did look big and impressive. This was their new family home and their new happy life that their mom had been telling them all about. The plan their mom had described was that both her and Heban, their daddy, would be running everything. Together they had big plans to make a lot of money while also making a wonderful new home for the kids.

Evelyn might have been hoping and thinking that with making this move to Indiana that things might possibly be better. Maybe this could turn out to be a lucky four-leaf clover opportunity, a fresh start.

It was a lot to take in, and Nancy started to feel slightly hopeful just listening to the excitement in her mother's voice. She wanted to feel hopeful and excited too, but she held back. She just could not trust this, at least not yet. She really had felt for a long time now that it was not safe to trust in anything, even her mother. But she kept still and kept what she was thinking to herself.

In the time leading up to this big move, there had been a lot of discussion from Heban and Evelyn about all of this and that life in Indiana was going to be something special. They painted a nice picture of how amazing this plan of theirs was going to turn out. But the dim light of hope that life might be better went dark within the very first day of moving in. The abuse they suffered while living at the farmhouse, sexual and physical, picked up again right where it had left off at the farmhouse.

When Heban came home from work at the gas station, the very first thing he did was to find Nancy. He would start looking for her in the house, outside, wherever. He continued looking, and when he found her, he would take her by her hand and lead her to his and her mother's bedroom. This time of day worked for him because Evelyn would be busy at work at the restaurant and unaware of what was going on at the house.

The year was 1966. Soon after the family had settled in, Nancy was enrolled in school for the fourth grade. Her sisters and brothers were also enrolled in their classes. Cynthia, the youngest of her sisters, would be going to kindergarten. Cynthia was extremely excited to be doing big things, just like her older sisters and brother. A school bus picked all the children up at the end of the driveway of their new house. This was exciting, and it was something they all talked about, and they were all were very much looking forward to.

Heban and Evelyn considered Nancy and her older sister Katie to be old enough to work in the restaurant and at the motel. Nancy had just turned ten, and Katie was thirteen. They were trained to wait on tables at the restaurant and wash dishes. A lot of the customers were truck drivers.

Their job at the motel when they were done working at the restaurant was to clean the rooms at the motel, and their work was always inspected.

The pond that was behind the house was not a nice swimming pond like the one they had been told about by their mother. This pond had old car parts floating in it, tires, logs, and other debris. The pond also had large snakes slithering and swimming around. Regardless, this is where Nancy learned to swim.

Heban took all the kids to the pond. He was going to teach all of them how to swim. Nancy was the very first one to learn. Heban's method of teaching you how to swim started with him dunking you and holding you under the water for a certain amount of time. He would decide how long to hold you under. Once you were able to survive that part of the swimming lesson, he then took you out to the deepest part of the pond. This was way out in the middle, quite a distance from shore. From there, in the middle of the pond, he would let go of you, and you were on your own. You either had to try to start swimming and paddling, or you just might drown. You needed to react quickly, think fast, and try your hardest to make it back to shore.

Fortunately, Nancy being strong-willed and determined, decided she was not going to drown. At least not that day, she thought. With every ounce of determination, she thrashed about, swallowing a lot of the dirty water, and eventually, she made it back to shore safely. She knew Heban took great pleasure in every day of his miserable life in hurting everyone. So, she did not trust for one single minute that he would care one bit if she should drown. Her siblings were all on the shore crying and begging, "Daddy, please help her. She's going to die." They were terrified that she was going to go under and never come back up. Heban made no effort at any time to help her.

The children were all standing on the shore, shaking

from what Nancy had just been through. They had just witnessed what Heban's cruel swim lesson looked like, and they were all completely terrified and traumatized.

CHAPTER THIRTEEN

MOVING TO INDIANA: MARIA

Maria remembers sharing a bedroom with her sisters at their new house in Indiana. She has fond memories of the love the kids all felt for each other and how they stuck up for each other. But the horrible memories are very much still there.

Maria was nine years old when they all moved to their new home in Indiana, leaving Ohio behind.

Beatings for all the children happened every single day. It did not matter about having a reason, a what for or a why; there was always something that Heban could find a reason for to beat them. The beatings he gave could be with a belt, a rubber hose, his boots, you never knew.

Sometimes you would just be sitting quietly on the couch, and he would pick up something, an object, and throw it at you. It could be a work boot. It could be any-thing. When their mom tried to step in to help or stop it, he would turn around with a mean and hateful look on his face and start beating on Evelyn until she was left lying on the floor helpless.

One day Heban dragged her by her hair to a wooded area behind the house. Everyone in the family was at the restaurant when this happened. Heban got mad, and he began grabbing and beating on all the kids. Evelyn stepped in to try and stop him, and he grabbed her by the hair and dragged her out of the restaurant and into the woods. He beat her that day half to death. Maria remembers her mother coming back from the woods, hours later with her nose bleeding and her mouth and eyes swollen. Maria was horrified at how bad her mother looked. She looked half-dead and like she was not going to make it. This was the punishment that she brought on herself for trying to step in and protect her children.

Whenever Heban beat the kids, he would whip them until they were bleeding, and then he would take them into the kitchen and pour salt on all their wounds and then dare them to scream.

Before leaving for school at breakfast one morning, Maria and Max were eating their cereal at the table when Max accidentally spilled his cereal on the floor. This made Heban mad, so he jumped up out of his chair and threw Maria's bowl of cereal on the floor too. Then Heban made both Max and Maria get down on the floor on all four like dogs and lick every bit of it up.

Maria's brothers and sisters all got caught smoking one time. Maria herself was not smoking, but she was with them at the time. When Heban asked if she was smoking too, she said that she was. Maria felt it was better to take a beating with all of them rather than having to hear and listen to their screams and cries. The kids always stuck together. They had made a pact. They said it helped to keep them as strong as possible under the circumstances. If one got in trouble, they would all say they had done it.

Max was caught more than once smoking that Maria can remember, but one day that sticks out is when Heban put him in a motel room and made him eat a whole carton of cigarettes as punishment. When he was done eating the cigarettes, he was then forced to drink salt water until he vomited.

After school, one day, Maria was doing her homework up in her bedroom when Heban yelled up and called her to come downstairs and said, "You come down here right now." Maria walked down the stairs, and Heban led her into his and her mother's bedroom and then closed the door behind them. The first thing that went through her mind was that he was going to beat her. Maria was standing in the room shaking when Heban opened the closet door and told her to get inside, and so she did.

At this time, Maria knew nothing about Heban sexually assaulting her sisters. Katie and Nancy both had been threatened not to tell anyone, and so they had not even told each other. Once Maria was inside the closet, Heban came inside with her and started reaching in and under her clothes and touching her all over. She had no idea what this was all about and what to expect or when he would stop. Maria was scared to death. Eventually, he did stop, and then he threatened her just like he had done with her sisters and her brother. He told her she had better keep her mouth shut and not tell anybody. He said, "If you tell anyone about this, your mother will go back to prison for the rest of her life, and your sisters and brother will all go to the orphanage."

When Maria turned eleven years old, her mother told her it was time for her to start working in the restaurant. At this age, her mother and Heban thought she was old enough. There were a lot of truck drivers that came into the restaurant every day for lunch. So, it was always busy. The first part of Maria's training was how to greet and serve water to customers. The second part was she needed to take out her order pad and ask the customers what they would like to order. Maria was scared to death to even walk out there. She had no confidence in herself, and she was afraid of the customers. She felt embarrassed too. She also felt stupid because she had been made to think that she was. She was called stupid by Heban all the time. Finally, her mom said, "Go on now, get out there; you will do fine." The first thing that Maria did was spill the water before she even made it to the table. The truck drivers that she was waiting on that day, fortunately, were genuinely nice about it. She managed to get out in a timid little voice, "Hi, my name is Maria." What she remembers next is that she dropped all of their salads on the floor. Feeling embarrassed and upset, she ran back to the kitchen crying and said to her mom, "Mommy, I can't do this." For this, Heban beat her for doing a bad job. She was not given a pass like, "Well, this was your first time," or "It is okay, you will do better next time." Instead, Heban said to her, "The next time, you will do it right, or you will keep getting a beating until you do get it right."

Thankfully, Maria's older sister Nancy was and still is a big help to her. She helped her to learn how to do better at the restaurant. Nancy taught Maria a lot of things. One of the most important things Nancy helped her with was becoming stronger. Maria absolutely needed to try to be stronger to survive.

Close to lunchtime one day, Maria and Max were arguing about something as all kids do, and Heban overheard it. It made Heban angry, and he yelled at them and accused them of acting like little babies. For acting like little babies, his punishment for them was that Maria had to take her shirt off, and they both had to get naked. He put them in a baby diaper that he took from his son Jacob's room. Once they had their diapers on, they were marched from the house up to the restaurant, and they were made to parade around in front of all the customers in their diapers. If they were going to act like babies, they would be treated like babies. Maria was about age twelve at that time, and her breasts were developed. She remembers how terribly mortified she was. To even talk or think about this now and to relive that day, for her, this was one of the worst days of her life. The embarrassment and shame she felt were overwhelming. She saw and felt all those truck drivers' eyes staring at her at the restaurant as she was made to parade around bear-chested and in a diaper. She thought and felt she could never ever show her face outside again. She was completely humiliated and ashamed.

For Maria, the thought of learning to swim was something she felt she could not survive. She had heard someone say that the pond looked to be about thirty feet deep at its deepest part. She felt she would never survive that and sink thirty feet down straight to the bottom. She was content to just hang around at the bank of the pond and play. You were not even allowed to dip your toes into the water if you had not taken the special dunking lesson from Heban. That lesson involved him holding you under the water until you were scared and breathless and then taking you out to the deep end of the pond and letting go of you. You either had to swim or sink to the bottom. Her older sisters Nancy and Katie had both learned how to swim, but Maria was just too terrified. She felt she was not as brave as her older sisters.

One day Max decided he wanted to try to learn how to swim. Heban dunked him, which was scary, and then he took him out to the deepest part of the pond, and he let him go. At the time, Max was about nine years old. Max started to doggie paddle, but he had a long way to go. Max started to scream and panic. Then he went under the water. Both Nancy and Katie wanted to jump in and swim out to help him, but Heban threatened them and said they were not allowed to help. Max popped up out of the water, but he was not going to make it. He was terrified, and he kept going back under the water. After what seemed like a long while and fearing Max was going to drown, Heban swam out to get him. Max was thrashing around and so scared that Heban slugged him to knock him out and then brought him back to shore. Max survived but just barely. Seeing all this scared Maria. Still to this day, she carries this memory of her brother almost drowning. She decided on that very day she never wanted to learn how to swim. Still to this day, she will not go near the water. Not even to dip her toes. She loves the warm sand at the beach, but she is terrified of the water. She can hardly stand to watch her grandkids when they are swimming. Panic takes over for her, and she relives this horrible day all over again. She fears her grand-children could go under while swimming and drown right in front of her.

It was Max's birthday, and the sisters all decided they wanted to bake him a cake. Maria lit the gas oven in the kitchen while Nancy and the others were mixing the cake ingredients together. Max's birthday is in July, so it happened to be a warm day outside, and they opened the kitchen windows. After mixing the cake and putting in the cake pans, Nancy carried them over to the oven. When she opened the door of the oven, it was still cold. The oven should have been ready by this time. So, Nancy lit a match to re-light the pilot light. When she did that, the gas had been on all that time, and it blew up in Nancy's face and body. She started running and screaming through the restaurant because she was on fire and burning. A waitress at the restaurant who knew and loved the kids quickly grabbed hold of Nancy and lifted and put her in the ice bin. Then she called for an ambulance, and Nancy was rushed to the hospital and admitted. Her condition was serious. The explosion and fire had burnt almost all of her hair off, and she was severely burned on her face, neck, and body.

Maria knew that she had lit the pilot light. She had done it many times before. The girls thought that the only possible explanation might be that the wind from the open windows might have blown the pilot light out while the gas was still on. It was an unfortunate and heartbreaking accident.

Evelyn went to the hospital to be with Nancy, but Heban would not allow her to stay with her. He said Evelyn had to get back to work at the restaurant. They had customers to take care of, and that was more important. So little Nancy was left alone at the hospital, afraid and in a lot of pain.

When Heban and Evelyn returned home from the hospital, Heban asked each of the kids who lit the oven. Maria admitted right off that she had lit it. She explained, saying, "I know I did." Because Heban felt it was her fault that Nancy was burnt, he burnt Maria's body with lit cigarettes while saying to her, "This is, so you know what it feels like to be burned."

After a bad beating one day, Maria felt more desperate than usual and called her real dad, crying to him on the phone and begging him to help her; she just could not take it anymore. When Heban found out that the kid's dad was coming because Maria had called him, he beat her so bad about the head that she could not hear out of either of her ears for several days. When her dad arrived to help and check on her, she had to sit on the couch and pretend that she was happy and that everything was okay. She had to say she had made a mistake by calling him. Nothing was wrong.

The same held true whenever the grandparents came over, Evelyn's dad and stepmother. You always had to act happy and keep your mouth shut, or Heban would beat you worse than the time before.

Maria did not have any friends at school either, just like her siblings. If you wanted to go to a ball game or a school activity, you needed to sleep with Heban first, and then you were allowed to go. If you were chosen by him and forced to ride with him in the car to go to the store, he would always pull off of the side of the road, and you had to let him touch you. The rides in the car were always dreaded by the girls.

Many nights the children were made to stay up all night redoing dishes or some other chore that they had failed to do right. There were many nights that this happened, and they never went to bed, and the next morning, they were expected and made to get dressed and go to school without a wink of sleep.

One time when both Heban and Evelyn went out of town for something, Mamaw told Heban when they returned that the girls Katie and Nancy had boys over, and they were smoking too. Having boys over was strictly forbidden. Nancy was fourteen, and Katie was sixteen. Heban asked both the girls if they had boys over while they were gone. Both denied that there were any boys in the house. Of course, he did not believe them. After all, his mother had told him that they did. Heban, believing they were lying to him, took them both to the basement and tied them each to a pole, and then he began to beat them. The beatings went on all throughout the day. When Maria returned home from school that day, and she got off the bus, she could see inside the basement windows. She saw her sisters were each tied up to poles, and they were crying. When Maria walked into the house, Heban confronted her and said, "I want you to tell me the truth. If you lie to me, the same thing will happen to you down in the basement." Maria said she looked Heban straight in his eyes and said her sisters were telling the truth, that there were no boys inside the house. Heban smacked her and said she was lying, and then he whipped her too. Heban went back to the basement and started beating Katie and Nancy all over again. Maria tried to cover her head to drown out the screaming and crying. The girls were kept down there for two or three days and were beat off and on during the day and night. Maria felt so helpless. She was overcome with the desperation of wanting to help, but there was nothing she could do. She feared they might die down there in that dirty dark basement. She said, "You are in a powerless situation, and you have no one to turn to. Everyone is afraid."

To this day, Maria has to walk out of a room when the TV news is on. Any news story about anything bad happening to anyone causes her to tremble and shake. She has a hard time even watching TV because many programs contain violence. If the TV is on and something bad is about to happen, or she even senses it will, or the music sounds like danger is coming, she moves herself to another room where she cannot see or hear any of it.

CHAPTER FOURTEEN

MOVING TO INDIANA: MAX

Max remembers the excitement he had about the new house they were moving to with the motel, restaurant, gas station, and repair garage. This move to their new home very soon became what he describes as a living hell. Even the pond his mother told him about where he could go fishing and swimming and have fun turned out to be a death trap. He felt that Heban had to be Satan himself. He ruled over everybody and everything. You lived in fear of him every minute out of every day.

One of Max's first work assignments after moving there was to go to their service station with Heban to clean it. Heban woke Max up one morning and said, "Get up; you have work to do." He told Max to sweep up the shop floor. Max was about ten years old. Heban handed him the broom and said, "Get at it, and I'll be back to check on your work." Heban then left Max there alone while he went to get a cup of coffee at the restaurant. When Heban returned sometime later, he looked all around the shop and inspected Max's work. As it always turned out the same way, Max had failed to do a good job. His work was not good enough, and Heban did not approve, so he smacked Max hard in the back of the head. Max looked at him and said, "Why did you do that?" Heban said, "You get down on your hands and knees, and you clean that dirt up around the legs of that bench, and I want every inch of this floor cleaned. Don't you dare stop until this is cleaned right, and I will be the one to tell you when it is right." Max was really scared as he dropped to the floor and started using his little bare hands and fingers to scrape away the dirt around all the edges and legs of the workbenches.

Most of all the family meals were food cooked at the restaurant. Each child would be served a plate of food, and it was not by their choice of what they were given to eat. If they left any food at all on their plate, maybe most likely because they did not like something, you were in for big trouble. The rule was hard and fast. You ate every single bite of food that was on your plate! If you did not, then whatever it was that was leftover on your plate would be saved for you. This was then served to you again for your next meal. You had to eat that leftover portion before you were allowed to eat anything else. Your plate would be left sitting out on the counter all day and then put in front of you at your next meal. You were not allowed anything additional until that plate of food was eaten. It did not matter if bugs crawled in it or on it or it became rancid. That plate of food had your name on it, and you would be eating it sooner or later. Max has memories of going to bed hungry many times because he could not bear to choke down the slop they had saved for him.

Cleaning was always a no-win situation. It was scary for everybody because it did not matter how hard you worked or how hard you tried Heban would find fault. It could be a piece of lint he found on the floor. A towel not folded right. This meant for all the kids that they would be beaten and then taken to the kitchen to have salt poured over their cuts. They were then told to start cleaning all over again, and they had better get it right this time.

Washing the dishes at the restaurant always came under the same harsh scrutiny. Maybe it was a spoon with a water spot found on it. This meant that every dish, utensil, pot, pan, everything would have to be washed again because of their careless and sloppy work by these stupid kids.

Max said beatings were given with water hoses, belts, switches, pieces of rubber. Sometimes he said his back was so bad he could not even stand the touch of a shirt on his back.

Max's beatings were awful, but it was more awful for him to witness the beatings his mom endured. One day he saw his mom up at the restaurant with a swollen black eye. Max asked what happened, and she said, "Nothing, honey, I fell, but I will be okay." Max did not believe her, and when he went back to the house, he told his sisters. All the kids had seen their mom hit, kicked, and thrown to the ground, and beat. Many times, it was because she had tried to step in to keep Heban from beating them. This always just made things worse for all of them.

After about a year and a half of living at the house and business, Heban came looking for Max. When he found him, he took him to his sisters' bedroom. The first thing he saw when Max walked through the door was his sister Nancy laying naked on her bed. Heban told Max to take his clothes off. Max looked at him and asked him why. Heban said, "It's because you are going to have sex with your sister." When Max shook his head and said no way, he did not want to do that, and he could not make him. Heban never hesitated for a minute, and he punched Max hard in the face and said, "You're going to do it anyway." When Heban had decided that Max was done, he pulled him off Nancy. Then Heban started beating Max bad enough to show he had suffered a beating. Heban had prepared a story for their mother. Heban told Evelyn that he caught Max sneaking around his sisters' bedroom, and when he found Max, he was in bed with Nancy having sex with her.

It was after this day that his sisters told Max that Heban had been sexually molesting them for quite a long time. Each of them had been keeping quiet about everything, just as Heban had told them they had to. His threat hung over them, and they were all afraid of him. They did not want their mom to go back to prison. They did not want to be separated from each other and taken to an orphanage.

Max being forced to have sex with his sisters was also what Heban called his insurance policy. If one of the girls were to ever get pregnant, Max would be the one to take the blame.

These forced sex acts happened all the time. You never knew when you would get the look or the command.

Max was worried for his sister Nancy. Max would ask Nancy about the car rides that Heban forced her to go on when they went to pick up his medicine. Heban had suffered a broken back from an accident years before, and he took a lot of drugs and narcotics for pain. Max would ask Nancy to tell him what happened on the car trips, but she was afraid to say anything, so she denied anything happened or that anything was wrong. Nancy hated those rides.

One day Max got into the liquor cabinet at the house. He knew full well if he got caught, it would not turn out good for him. But for whatever reason, he decided he wanted to at least have a taste. After more than possibly a few swallows, he started feeling funny and even swaying and staggering. Heban happened to come back to the house and saw him staggering about. Heban asked him what was wrong, and Max replied that he just did not feel good. Max wanted to pass it off as having the flu. Heban called him a liar and said, "So you want to drink, okay you are going to drink" He took Max down into the basement and made Max drink until he finally passed out. Then Heban left him alone in the dark basement to sleep it off. When Max woke up, he climbed up the stairs, and when he got to the top of the stairs, Heban made him go back down. Max began to cry and told Heban he was afraid because there were mice and rats down there, and it was dark. It did not matter. Heban made him spend the night in the dark in the basement, sick, alone, and afraid.

Another time Max snuck a cigarette to smoke. He just wanted to try it. Unfortunately, Heban's mother caught him, and she told Heban. Heban asked Max right out if he had been smoking, and Max lied and said he was not. Heban then told him that his mother saw him smoking, and she had told him that she saw him, so he then said to Max, "So are you calling my mother a liar? Tell the truth," so Max did admit that he did try to smoke just one cigarette. Heban took Max to the basement and tied him to a metal pole, and beat him for this.

Another time Max got caught smoking, and Heban took him to one of the motel rooms and made him take off all his clothes. He then took him outside on the side of one of the buildings. Heban knew Max would not run off because he was naked. Heban left for a short while and came back with an arm full of cigarettes, chewing tobacco, and cigars. He made Max smoke just the filters of several packs of cigarettes. Next, he made him chew and swallow the chewing tobacco. Then he had to smoke several cigars. Heban then made him start drinking saltwater. Max heaved so hard, and for so long, he felt like he was going to die.

Because of all the abuse, mental, sexual, and physical, Max started rocking more in his bed at night. This is not considered to be a serious disorder by many medical professionals. Professionals report that sometimes this is simply a way to deal with stress. It can be for some soothing and relaxing. But Max's rocking in bed at night made Heban angry because he could hear him rocking from his bedroom. Heban would angrily barge into Max's room and start smacking Max in the face to wake him up, and he would yell at him and tell him to stop rocking. That he had better knock it off. Some nights Heban would come into Max's bedroom two or three times and smack him hard. Many times, Heban would then yank him out of his bed and stand Max in the corner for the rest of the night. Max got so good and spent so much time in the corner he was able to learn how to sleep while standing up. After many a night of standing in the corner all night long, he was made to get dressed in the morning and go to school.

Even for Christmas and the holidays, there are no good memories for Max. One year he did get a hot wheel race-track from Santa. He was wild with excitement about that gift, and it was completely unexpected. What boy would not be excited? But the thrill and excitement did not last long. Heban told him and the other kids to pick up and put all their toys away. Heban had decided that they were done playing. Max does not remember for what reason if he was not moving fast enough or what he might have possibly done wrong, but what he does remember is that Heban got up and grabbed parts of his racetrack and started hitting him with the pieces until the track was broke. Then after Max's Christmas present was completely broken, Heban ordered Max to go to his bedroom for the rest of the day.

Max shared that there were no good memories for him when they lived in Indiana. This was not the paradise that his mom had said it would be. For Max, this was more like what Satan's hell and a torture chamber would be.

One day Heban had a man with him who had come out to fish in the pond. Max had never seen this man before. They had a small rowboat, and Heban put Max in the boat with them. Max thought they were all going to go out and fish together. Heban rowed the boat out into the deepest area of the pond. Then Heban just stood up in the boat and grabbed Max and threw him in the water. Then Heban paddled the boat away from Max. Max right away started screaming for help, and Heban said, "You can either learn to swim right now, or you are going to drown." Max frantically doggy paddled himself to shore and tried to rest there for a minute, but Heban made him get back into the boat, and he took him right back out to the deepest part of the pond and threw him in again. He repeated this a few more times. Max remembers and believes that when it was not fun for Heban any longer in front of his friend, he finally stopped.

One day Heban's kids from his first marriage were visiting. They were all headed into town for ice cream. Heban had three kids from his first marriage. Max asked if he could go along too because he liked ice cream. Heban laughed and said, "No, you don't get to go for ice cream. Nobody invited you. Now get up to your bedroom and get your room cleaned."

The house they lived in was built over a live spring. This meant that often the basement would fill up with water. One day Max was arguing with one of his sisters. Heban started yelling at Max, and he accused Max of talking back to him. For this back talk, if, in fact, it even was back talk, Heban took Max to the basement. He then tied Max's hands and arms behind his back and tied his body to one of the metal poles, and left him down there. It was raining that day and had been raining the day before, so the basement was starting to fill up with water. As Max was tied up, he could see the water rising, and he started screaming out, saying, "Daddy, the water is getting high; the basement is filling up." It was dark, cold, and wet, and he was terrified. Heban left him tied to that pole all day. His sister Maria waited for the right time and snuck down with a sandwich which she had made to feed to Max. His hands and arms were tied behind his back, so she planned to feed him. Maria waded through the water that was by that time knee-deep on her. After she fed Max, Maria had just got back up to the top of the stairs when Heban opened the door and saw her. He yelled, "What are you doing?" Maria told Heban all she was doing was just checking on Max to be sure he was okay, and so he let her pass by him, and then he shut the door. The water kept rising, and when it was up to Max's neck, he started panicking. Max saw a snake swimming toward him, and he screamed, "Daddy, daddy, there is a snake, please daddy help me." Soon Heban appeared with a gun, and he shot the snake in front of Max's face. Max has relived this nightmare in his mind repeatedly, and he cannot believe he was not hurt with buckshot from the rifle or drowned or bitten by the snake. He really did not expect to survive that day. Every minute that passed for him while he was tied to the pole and the water was filling up, he felt death was near. Heban was going to let him die down there.

Another close call for Max was the day that Heban was angry because Max had brought him the wrong part while he was working on a car repair in their shop. Heban sent Max to go and get the right part. When Max was not returning fast enough, Heban got mad and jumped into his

143

wrecker tow truck, and sped off to find him. Heban was in a rage, and he drove straight at Max to purposely hit him. Max saved himself by jumping into a ditch and out of the path of the tow truck. To this day, Max believes that Heban had every intention of hitting and killing him. He believes Heban would have said it was an accident.

One Christmas, Heban got a 30-30 rifle for Christmas. For some unknown reason, Heban was mad at Max and said to him that he was going to kill him with his new rifle. Max was scared that he was serious, so he called his grandfather, his mother's father. His grandpa told Max not to say anything but that he and Granny were coming. They would get there as fast as they could. They both came, and they acted like nothing was going on. They had cups of coffee, cool and calm as can be, and then Grandpa said to Heban, "Did you threaten to kill Max with your rifle?" Of course, Heban denied it. Max's Grandpa took the gun and broke the butt of it on the porch floor, and then he told Heban," If you lay one hand on that boy, I will be back." Grandpa was Max's hero right then. After they left, Heban asked Max how Grandpa knew about the gun and what he had said, and Max said, "I do not know." Hearing that, Heban threatened to beat everyone in the family until he found out how Grandpa found out. Max could not let that happen to his family, so he said that he had been the one that had called because he was scared that Heban was going to kill him. Heban beat Max to a pulp that day and then threatened that if he called and told his grandpa about it, he would beat him again.

Max feels that his grandpa really loved him. He was the only male that ever stood up for him. The kids' real father was called a few times by the kids begging him for help. And when their dad was not in jail, he would come. But it never turned out the way the kids wanted it to. Their picture of hope was all of them piling in their dad's car with their mom and him driving them away to safety. He was coming to rescue them. But what would really happen is Heban would shoot his gun at their dad's car, accuse him of being a dead-beat father, and he would threaten the kids to keep their mouths shut about everything or suffer the worst beating of their life.

Whenever Max tried to rescue his mom from a beating, it only made things worse for both of them.

Heban had friends who also kept a watchful eye over Evelyn to make sure she never tried to make a run for it with the kids.

One of the last nightmares for Max while living in Indiana happened after there was a fire and the family had lost the motel, restaurant, and house. They were left with just the garage. Heban and his mother brought in two trailers and parked them on the lot to live in. Heban started running card games and gambling in the back of the garage to help make some money, and he hired a prostitute named Jeanie to live in the back room of the garage. Jeanie was available for the truck drivers, and Heban would make a large cut from her services. She was also available to Heban, free of charge, whenever he wanted. One day Heban told Max that he had to have sex with Jeanie. He said it was because he wanted Jeanie to teach him some stuff. Max did what he was told, and after that, Heban asked Jeanie in front of Max how he did. He asked if Max had learned anything. Jeanie told Heban that Max would be all right and he would do fine when he got a little older. Heban then grabbed Max by his arm, and they went to the trailer to find the youngest daughter Cynthia. Heban forced Max to have sex with her. After Max did, then, Heban forced himself on Cynthia. Max is not sure how old she was then, but she may have been eight or nine.

These memories have haunted Max for many years and have left him with hate for himself and for an awfully long time thinking his sisters hated him too for what he was forced to do.

Max nervously shutters inside whenever he sees a canister of salt. The stinging pain and hurt all come rushing back.

All this makes you wonder. How could this have possibly happened to these poor kids? How were they able to survive? Each of the kids shared their own story with the same details. They lived it. They saw it. They suffered it. It happened.

CHAPTER FIFTEEN

MOVING TO INDIANA: CYNTHIA

Cynthia was excited about going to kindergarten when they moved to Indiana. She was going to ride the big school bus to school just like her older brother and sisters.

When school was over for her, at the end of the day, her daddy, Heban, would come to pick her up and drive her home. She would not be taking the bus home every day. Every day her daddy would bring her a fresh bowl of peaches for her to eat while riding in the car home. While Cynthia was enjoying eating her fresh bowl of peaches, Heban would reach inside her panties as she sat next to him. Cynthia, just like her brother and sisters, was told to keep this their little secret. This was special just for her. Cynthia was five years old when this started. For all, she knew this is what happened with all little girls when their daddies picked them up from school.

Whenever Cynthia was bad or when all the kids were being whipped and punished for something, she would get so scared that without fail, she would wet her pants. For wetting her pants, she received an extra beating. Wetting your pants meant you were a bad little girl.

Cynthia remembers the day well that Max and Maria had to wear a diaper because Heban thought they were acting like babies. Her sister Maria had to go bear-chested up to the restaurant and parade around all the customers in a baby diaper. She also remembers on that day, the parking lot was filled full of Mayflower trucks. It was an extra busy day at the restaurant and a day that Maria has never recovered from. The shame and embarrassment Maria felt that day still haunts her. It felt worse than some of the beatings. She was made to parade around at the restaurant bear-chested with a diaper because Heban said she acted like a baby. Being made to expose her breasts was so humiliating to her it is beyond any words she can think of to describe this day.

Each day when the kids got home from school, they had their chores to do with the twenty-minute time limit set by Heban to complete whatever the chore might be. Every day you failed no matter how hard you tried. Every day you got a beating.

One day Cynthia accidentally broke a dish, and for that, she was backhanded so hard she fell against something in the kitchen and cut open the back of her head. Blood was streaming down her neck and back. Cynthia was not allowed to tell anyone about what and how it happened, and she was not taken to the hospital or seen by a doctor. She wears a nasty scar on the back of her head from it. The bleeding continued for a long time, and she wondered after seeing all the blood on her and everywhere if she was going to die.

Cynthia, like her sister Maria, never learned to swim. Because you were not allowed in the water unless you let Heban dunk you, learning to swim was just too scary for her. She was there standing on the shore of the pond the day her brother Max almost drowned. She heard his terror and screams as he kept going under the water and fighting desperately to keep from drowning. Cynthia was afraid that Heban would be just as happy if she did drown so, she chose to never take that risk. To this day, Cynthia is still afraid of the water and has no desire to be around water.

Cynthia hated it when Heban would barge into the bathroom while the girls were taking their baths or getting dressed. It always felt like he was staring at you from somewhere. When Cynthia and her sister Maria were taking their turn for baths, they always felt like Heban was outside in the dark watching everything through the window screen.

Cynthia shared a story about one of Heban's money-making schemes was to have an accident in the car while Evelyn and the kids were in it too because you would get more settlement money for injured children. Heban would claim that another car had run him off the road. It was not his fault. In one accident, Evelyn was hurt so bad that she was in traction for her neck and back. Heban's mother was so mean to Evelyn she would walk by her and pull her up by her hair until she screamed. Heban's mother was mad because she had to work more at the restaurant while Evelyn was recuperating.

At school, Cynthia was called "Lonely Girl" by the other kids. She got this label because she was not allowed to have friends. Heban's rule and reason were that the kids might tell friends about their home life. No friends, girlfriends, or boyfriends allowed. So, Cynthia ate lunch alone and sat by herself when outside for recess. She did at one point make a friend at school, and she kept it a secret from her mom and Heban. Cynthia saw and watched a little girl who no one else wanted to be friends with. This poor little girl had been burnt and badly scarred in a fire. Both of her parents had died in the fire, and they had lost everything.

The little girl's name was Millie. Millie's face and arms and legs were burnt so bad it was hard to even look at her. The other kids made fun of her and called her ugly names. But for Cynthia, she felt love for Millie and wanted to be her friend. The two little girls had something in common. A lot of hurt and pain, and loneliness in their lives. Together they were happier.

Cynthia was allowed to attend church sometimes with her younger brother Jacob. Her older sisters and brother never had this chance. They did not know about God's love and praying. The only time they heard about Jesus was when they went to Bible school one week out of the year.

One year at Bible school, the kids learned a song, "Peter, James, and John." It was a catchy tune about being out on the deep blue sea and catching some fishies. Max would sing the song at the top of his lungs because it made him feel good to know the words and to hear his own voice. But Heban hated it when he heard him singing, and so he would smack Max in the mouth to make him stop.

Jacob was Heban's and Evelyn's son that they had together after they moved to Indiana. Jacob was always treated like a little prince. For Cynthia to have the privilege of going to church with Jacob made her feel special. A member of the Methodist church picked them up and brought them back home after Sunday school. Sunday School is where Cynthia learned about God, faith, and prayer. She learned that God loved her. She needed to feel loved. Cynthia would lie in bed at night and fold her hands and pray for her mother, siblings, her friend Millie, and herself.

For all the nights that she heard her brother Max being smacked and whipped for rocking in his bed, she would fold her hands and pray to God to please help her brother Max. She would raise her tiny fists in the air and pray harder. Cynthia became the prayer warrior for her mother and siblings.

Cynthia felt bad for her brother Max because he never caught a break. Her memory is that every single day of his life, Max was beaten for something.

Cynthia knew the rules well. You were to be seen and not heard as a child. As a child, you had nothing to say that mattered. If adults came to visit, you were not allowed to be seated with them. You needed to stay off in the distance and keep your mouth shut. You had better keep your mouth shut, or you knew what would happen.

Close to Christmas one year, the children's real father, Billie, and his wife came to visit the kids. Cynthia remembers that her gift was a new dress they had picked out special for her. But the size they got was too big for her. It was discussed and decided that the dress would be given to one of her sisters, and Billie and his wife said, "Come on, Cynthia, go get in the car. We are going to take you to town right now and buy you a dress that fits. It's for Christmas, and we want you to have your present from us." This announcement immediately made Heban mad, and he stood up and ordered Billie and his wife to get out of his house. He yelled, "She is going nowhere and especially not with you. Get out of my house now, or I am going to kill you both." Billie and his wife could not believe what was happening and headed for the door and their car. Once they were in the car, Heban took his rifle and started shooting at the car as they tried to drive away. Billie was shocked by what had happened, and he reported it to the local police. But nothing ever came of it for whatever reason.

School was a refuge and something Cynthia looked forward to every day. One day she chewed off the eraser from the end of her pencil and started using the metal on the pencil head to dig into the wood on the top of the desk. The teacher saw what she was doing and sent her to the office to see the principal. While in the office, the school counselor or helper asked her if she had trouble at home and if she did would she like to talk about it. The counselor said that children that act out like this usually have something going on at home. Cynthia knew from the rules that Heban set down you had better keep your mouth shut, or you would be sure to get a beating. And, after he beat you, he would beat your mother and siblings. There was also the chance you would be taken to the orphanage, and your mother would go back to prison for the rest of her life. She looked down at the floor and shook her head no, that nothing was wrong at home.

When the school called her mom and Heban about what had happened, Heban decided the appropriate punishment would be for her to eat a full box of erasers and swallow them. She was so sick after that she could hardly hold her head up.

Cynthia grew up to be a very patient person. She had to wait through all her childhood to be free of Heban's abuse. Her daily prayers gave her hope to stay patient and wait on the lord. She knew from the Bible "That this too shall pass." She knew one day she would be able to walk out that door and be free of him.

There were locks on the refrigerator and cabinets that had food in them. You were not allowed food in between your meals. At school, they had to pay for their lunches. This was hit or miss for all the kids. Some days, the children had money for lunch, and some days they went hungry.

Heban was also stingy with the money when it came to buying clothes and shoes for Evelyn and the kids. Shopping for school clothes at Goodwill one time, Cynthia got a new pair of shoes which were really an old pair of shoes that had been donated to the Goodwill store.

She remembers being in disbelief that these shoes were chosen for her by her mother, and they were going to be her new shoes just because they fit her. Someone had completely cut the toes out of the top of the shoes. On the way to the store, she had been all excited. That quickly changed. She knew the kids would laugh at Lonely Girls' shoes. Heban had only given their mother $20.00 to buy used clothes and shoes for all five children.

The kids were always told what a no-good person their real father was. They were told he did not pay child support and he did not care or love them at all. When Cynthia lived with him for a few short months because she ran away, her real father had a suitcase full of receipts as proof that he did. He worked on the railroad, and the support had been deducted from his paycheck to pay for his five children.

One morning, much to their surprise, the kids saw a box of powdered doughnuts in the kitchen. The very first thing Nancy did was lick the powdered sugar off every single doughnut. That did not bother the rest of the kids one bit. Each kid grabbed a couple of those wet and sticky dough- nuts and chowed down on them. This was still a special treat even if Nancy had licked all the powdered sugar off.

Even though Max and Jacob shared a bedroom, it was Max's responsibility to keep everything clean. If Jacob made a mess, Max was in trouble. Jacob was treated like a king by both Evelyn and Heban. He could do no wrong. You would think that the other kids would have resented Ja- cob, but just the opposite, they adored him. They protected and loved him. They did not want him to suffer as they did. They would even take the blame for him no matter what he did.

For the food left on their plates because they could not stomach to eat it, at one point in time, Max found a secret solution. One day he showed his sisters a little trap door he found on the floor of the kitchen. The kids used this trap door space to scrape their uneaten food into. It probably ended up being dinner for one of the big rats that lived with them.

A fun project came about when all the kids decided to build an outside playpen for their little brother Jacob. They went around to abandoned houses and used the wood lying around from those old houses. This outdoor playpen was huge, and Jacob played in it for hours.

One day when Cynthia was living with her real dad, she rode her bike to her mom's sister's house, her aunt Elizabeth's, to see her cousins. She was excited to tell her granny all about her visit and spending time with one of her cousins. When she told Granny about this, she told Cynthia that those were not her real cousins, and she should never go there again. Cynthia does not know why she said that. But it raised the still unanswered question of why she tried so hard to keep the families apart.

Cynthia's memories of abuse are still painful. One of the worst memories for her was the day that she was getting off the school bus and heard her sisters Katie and Nancy screaming and crying from the basement windows. She peeked through the basement windows and could see they were tied up to poles in the basement. Heban was yelling while beating them. What brought this on was Heban's mother told Heban that the girls had boys over and that they were smoking. Heban and Evelyn had been out of town for a few days. The beatings went on for three full days and nights. It is a memory you cannot erase no matter how hard you try.

If you accidentally spilled your food, you ate it off the floor. Cynthia was eating a piece of French toast, and the French toast went flying when Heban smacked her for something. That made him madder, so he made her get down on the floor like a dog and eat the French toast off the floor and then lick the floor clean.

One of the insurance claim accidents was an accident with the tow truck wrecker. Cynthia and Jacob were in the wrecker with their mom. Evelyn ended up in traction; she was hurt so bad. She was in traction for a while, and so Heban was angry about that and would beat her. She was not able to work at the restaurant and help with the kids. She was worthless. Heban's mother was mad too because she had to work harder. She would yank hard and pull on Evelyn's hair to make her cry whenever she walked by her.

Whenever Heban's medicine started to run low, his rage intensified.

Their mom did try to escape several different times, but there were people Heban had watching her. Evelyn and the kids would all be in the car, packed and ready to make their getaway, when suddenly a semi-truck would pull up and block their path. Or Heban would appear out of nowhere. It was as though there were eyes on them watching all the time.

Sometimes Heban would load all the kids in the car and tell them he was taking them to an orphanage just to scare them. Just to hear them cry and beg him to let them stay.

Cynthia cannot stand to be yelled at for anything. It is upsetting for her. She shares that she would rather be hit or smacked than yelled at.

At age ten or eleven, Cynthia started acting out. Not the smartest thing for her to do but one day, she decided to run away. She was found, and she told Heban and her mom that she did not want to live with them anymore. Much to her surprise, when she said she wanted to go live with her real dad, her mother and Heban drove her to her grandfather's house and dropped her off. Her dad came to pick her up the next day. The only reason she thinks that they let her go is that both her mom and stepdad were in some legal trouble about this time. Heban had forced her mother to steal a prescription pad at the doctor's office to fill out his own prescriptions for his drugs. He told her he would break her hand if she did not steal it. Cynthia also thought they had been possibly accused of stealing some money, but she is not sure about the details on that, and her oldest sister had called the police on Heban and accused him of breaking into her house after she was married and raping her. So, the truth of the matter was they did not need another daughter talking to the police or being reported as a runaway. They needed to get out of town and out of the state.

On the day for the next move, which was Kentucky, a big U-Haul van showed up at Cynthia's real dad's house to pick her up. She did not want to leave her dad, but she was not given a choice, and her mother had custody. She would have rather lived with a drunk father that loved her than the devil who wished the very worst for her, her siblings, and her mother. They were all supposed to meet her mother and sisters at the Ohio and Kentucky line. From there, they would drive to their new home in the hills of Kentucky. They had lived in Indiana for seven years. From 1966 to 1973.

CHAPTER SIXTEEN

MOVING TO INDIANA: KATIE

Katie describes Heban as a man that had such a mean look that it scared you clear through to your bones.

The rules for Katie and her sister Nancy were no short skirts and no dresses. Katie was thirteen when they moved to Indiana and started school there. They were also not allowed to have a boyfriend or go out on a date until they were sixteen. By the time Katie was sixteen and starting to date, Heban would follow her and her date and spy on them. It was not fun for her, and it was scary for her dates. Boys were deathly afraid of Heban. It was hard for the girls to be asked to school dances and other school events for that reason. Heban had a reputation, and nobody wanted to upset him.

When Katie was allowed to attend a school dance or what they called a sock hop, Heban would show up there too. It was so embarrassing for her. He would stand against the wall inside the gym and just glare at her. If he lost track of her because she left to use the bathroom, immediately when they got home, he would check her panties to see if she had sex with anybody.

It did not matter what the chores were or the work that the kids had to do at the restaurant and motel; it never met Heban's standards. It did not matter how hard you tried; it was foolish to ever think that maybe at least one time Heban would tell you that you had done a good job. It just never ever happened. Heban told the kids repeatedly that they were all just too stupid and no good for anything brats that could not do anything right.

Heban would go to the kitchen drawer and yank it open and start inspecting the silverware. He would find one spoon with a water spot on it, and this would throw him into a wild rage. Then the next thing you heard and saw was him dumping the entire silverware drawer on the floor and taking out all the dishes, pots, pans, and throwing all that on the floor too. Then you would hear him yelling and demanding that all of us stupid little kids get in the kitchen and wash and dry and put away everything that was on the floor. He would then add, and this time, you had better do it right. When he inspected everything again, and he supposedly found one tiny water spot, all of this would start all over again after beating them. Some nights they never went to bed. Some nights they got dressed and went to school without ever having a wink of sleep.

Katie said Heban's parents moved in with them. At first, she said Heban's mother was nice, but that did not last long. She enjoyed tattling on the kids and then watching with delight the beating he gave them. Papaw, Heban's father, was a terrible drunk, and Heban took great pleasure in beating him all the time. Papaw would swear and yell at him the whole time, and Heban would beat him then, all the harder.

Jacob, Heban, and Evelyn's little boy could say whatever he wanted, and he would never get backhanded. He was a mouthy little guy and was always babied. Katie still loved him, but she also felt resentment because it was not fair. He must have been loved, and since they were beaten all the time, the only conclusion had to be that they were not loved.

Katie, being the oldest, always felt it was her responsibility to try and protect her younger brother and sisters. She had always felt that way. There were times Katie called the sheriff's department and reported the abuse. They never believed the kids. They always thought the wild stories they told had to be lies. They would say it was too farfetched. Nobody could be as evil and do all those kinds of things to children. You would have to be a monster. So, there was never any help from teachers, judges, sheriffs, or family. At that time, Heban and their mother were well known and respected in the community. This was only because no one could see behind closed doors.

Even aunt Elizabeth and Granny and Grandpa did not believe them. Or at least for most of it. Part of the reason is that Evelyn fearing for all their lives, felt it was safer to stay and lie than to suffer what could happen if she told the truth about everything. So, if Evelyn's family asked her about what the kids were saying, she would say they were lying. Getting anyone to help was hopeless. So, life for most of the time felt completely hopeless and that things would never change.

Katie said her mom later in life denied that she knew about a lot of things that were going on. Katie said her mom had her reasons for the way things were, and she is gone now, so as far as she is concerned, what good does it do to blame her. It will not take away or erase any of the pain, ugliness, or nightmares.

By the time Katie was sixteen, she had married just to be able to get out of the house. Still worried about her siblings, she went to see an attorney to get advice one day.

She asked what would happen to her if she killed Heban. What would happen to her if she mutilated him, she asked. The answer the attorney gave her, and even the next attorney said that what most likely would happen is she would end up going to prison. That answer was not what she had hoped for, so she decided there had to be another way to try and make all this stop.

Even though Katie lived in an apartment with her husband Joseph, every day, Heban would come knocking on the door. He knew when Joseph was working. Katie told her husband, and he told her not to let him in. He said just do not answer the door. Heban would try stopping at different times during the day and try the door handle. If by mistake it was unlocked, he would come in unannounced and force himself on her even though she was married. As far as he was concerned, he still owned her.

After being married for a while, Katie and her husband, Joseph, had a little boy. This was an incredibly happy time for Katie. She loved this little baby with all her heart, and she was a wonderful and loving mother. Her siblings stopped by often to play and love on this bundle of happiness. The baby's name was Little Joe. He was a beautiful, warm, and a wonderful gift from heaven.

At eighteen months old, Little Joe suddenly died. It turns out he had an exceedingly rare blood disease. Katie was so distraught over his death that she attempted suicide three different times. She and her husband had divorced before Little Joe died.

Katie became increasingly worried for her siblings because things for them at home were getting worse. She desperately felt, as the oldest child, she needed to figure out a way to help them. She decided on faking a break-in at her apartment and calling the police. Her plan was to tell them Heban broke in and raped her. His arrest and conviction for breaking and entering and rape should put him away for an awfully long time, she hoped. This was her plan.

She says that she was not an incredibly good criminal, so some of her plans did not turn out the way she had hoped. She followed through staging the break-in right after Heban made one of his forced visits. She called the police after he left and made the report. The story hit all the newspapers. This was big news on a slow news day. The story alone affected Heban's and Evelyn's reputation in the community. Heban never served a day in jail; the case fell apart. But it did expose the whole family coupled with other things that had recently come to light. Most people were afraid of Heban, so for most of the years living there in Indiana, nobody asked any questions. But now people were talking. Soon the town folk quit coming around, so they lost more customers. They were going broke. There had been a fire at the restaurant, motel, and house, burning it to the ground sometime earlier, which had hurt them financially. They had made a makeshift operation, but it was not the same. Some of those details are vague in the kid's memory. They do remember living in trailers that were hauled in on the property. What they recall the most is the hard times for everyone.

The chapter for them in Indiana was over. Heban's side of the family, aunts, uncles, and cousins lived in Kentucky, so he decided that would be their next move.

If there was any insurance money from the fire, the kids were never told. But Heban and Evelyn were able to secure a loan in Kentucky to buy land to build a new home. Heban was a mastermind at controlling everything and everyone around him to get what he wanted. Such powers and influence he had, and he used all of it for evil.

Katie did not make the move with the rest of her family to Kentucky. She tells with great sadness that her mother did not even tell her that they were moving. On the day of the move, her mother, Heban, and the kids were packed up and ready to pull out of the driveway when her mother called her to say goodbye. Katie stayed on living in Indiana until 1975.

Katie shared that she cannot recall even just one good memory from her childhood. A childhood filled with pain, hurt, and the never-ending feeling of hopelessness.

CHAPTER SEVENTEEN

EPILEPSY

Elizabeth's husband and my dad died at the young age of only thirty-nine in August of 1970, leaving behind his wife and three children. Owen had decided that he did not want to live anymore. My mother, Elizabeth was in the kitchen cooking dinner for the family, and he was standing beside her peeling potatoes. He left the kitchen as though he was going to be right back and went into his bedroom. He took out his hunting rifle from the bedroom closet and sat on the side of the bed. He propped it firmly between his knees and pointed it at his stomach. He then cocked it and pulled the trigger. His youngest daughter heard the shot and rushed to her parent's bedroom and found her dad slumped across the bed and covered in blood. Owen was rushed to the hospital by ambulance and died a few hours later while on the operating table.

Owen had planned his suicide days before, but no one in our family saw the possible signs or suspected it. After the funeral service, all of us in the family started looking back over the weeks before his death. He had his only suit dry cleaned. He went to the barbershop and got a haircut. He spent special time and shared some advice with his children the night before he took his life. I cannot remember for sure, but I think that he left the family a note. I know he had expressed that he felt his family would be better off without him. Because he could not hold a job because of his seizures, he felt he was just a financial burden.

While my mom's younger sister Evelyn was living in Indiana and trying to survive the hell she and her children were suffering, Elizabeth's husband Owen and their lives with their children were going through turbulent and tragic times too. I was Elizabeth and Owen's oldest daughter, and I had left home and married at eighteen just to get out of the house. This was much like what my mother had done when she was just sixteen years old.

I did not want to get married. I actually drove in the opposite direction of the church with my maid of honor in the car because I did not want to go through with it. I really wanted to get a job and go to work and hopefully save some money for college. But living at home was getting harder and harder. So many young girls feel that if they get married, all their troubles will go away, and they will live that happily ever after dream. The princess fairy tale story that little girls grow up reading and believing. What is true many more times is that you are just trading one bad home situation for another bad home situation. Girls rushing off to get married hoping they will live happily ever after is not the best plan.

As a teenager, I had drifted away from the church during my high school years. The church I attended while growing up had rules about music, makeup, movies, dancing, and others. I was not aligned with all their thinking and beliefs. It seemed too strict for a teenage girl who wanted to date. It did not occur to me to seek out a different church with different beliefs. I just stopped going. Years later, I felt that with everything that had been going on at home, if I would have turned to the church for some of the answers and guidance, perhaps some things might have turned out differently.

Our dad Owen had been suffering from epilepsy seizures for most of his married life. Early in the marriage, the seizures were mild but then got progressively worse. Some of the seizures he had at work and sometimes while driving the car, which was extremely dangerous. His seizures started somewhere around late 1952. So, from about that time until he died in 1970, Owen and all of us in the family lived through this daily struggle. There was never a warning for when the next seizure and attack might happen.

The history timeline for epilepsy shares that early on, the medical professionals treated epileptic patients as being lunatics, crazy, or possessed. That stigma followed them for many years. Then experimental studies were conducted, some of which were terribly harmful and painful to the patients. Later, there were some advances made in the pathology of the disease and the connection that epilepsy had with various psychiatric symptoms. These patients were not crazy or mentally ill. Their disease could be controlled. They could live normal productive lives with the proper experienced medical care and proper drugs.

It was just bad timing for our dad, Owen. He had been born in an era and time before the right drugs and treatments were available, and he was unfairly labeled as someone suffering from mental illness. He was exhibiting some symptoms, but you could not rule out the fact that the numerous experimental electric shock treatments to his brain coupled with experimenting with multiple combinations of different drugs over a long period of time did not worsen his condition. Elizabeth and Owen lived in a small town, and so there were not any top medical experts in the area available to them. He was medically treated as a human guinea pig. Elizabeth and Owen's mother, Sara Ann, took the advice of the doctors without question because that is what they thought was best. Back then, people did not question their doctors. If the doctor said you needed surgery, you had it. You did not hear about getting second opinions or seeing a specialist. Your doctor was your doctor for everything, from delivering a baby to amputating your foot.

Today many epileptic patients are leading full productive, and happy lives. Thank goodness for the major advances the medical profession has made with this disease.

Because of the seizures, Owen was not able to hold a job. To most employers, he was considered a liability and a danger. He could have a seizure at any time. His not being able to work posed a money shortage issue for the family. It also obviously affected his manhood because he was not able to be the man of the house and support his family. He drank to drown out his sadness and low self-esteem, and then he took out his anger on his family and everyone around him. The children did not always feel loved, and it was difficult for them at times to love back.

At one point, Owen was committed to a mental hospital

because of his frightening behavior. It was heartbreaking for me to visit him and see how much he was suffering. I would visit him often at the mental hospital, taking him milkshakes and treats to cheer him up. I often witnessed the patients being treated badly. It was shocking to see the inhumane treatment of these helpless patients. I never saw compassion from the staff. Maybe their job was hard. My dad begged me to please help him get out. It broke my heart. My hands were tied. I had no legal rights to do anything. I could not even question his care. I strongly felt that even though he had been mean to me, he was still my father. I would have to be a monster to not hurt and feel sad watching him suffer like that. I prayed that he would get better.

If he had not taken his own life and had hung on to hope just a little while longer, perhaps a few years, things might have turned out a lot different for him. A few years after his death, there were major research developments made for epilepsy and some major improvements in drug therapies that medical professionals were using.

I volunteered for a short time with a friend at the local Epilepsy Foundation, years after my own family was grown. The fundraising events I helped with featured many speakers who had epilepsy. They told many success stories. With the advances available in modern medicine, many can now live productive and happy lives.

For my dad, "I wish that you could have lived at this later time so that you too could have been happy and productive and had a better life."

CHAPTER EIGHTEEN

MY HIGH SCHOOL CLASS TRIP

One day that stands out in my memory dates back to the summer of 1968. I was seventeen years old, and I was attending my high school's end-of-the-school-year class trip. Our class voted on and planned a day at a large amusement park. This amusement park had some of the best roller coasters in the country, so it was a popular place to go. I was excited and looking forward to this day even though I was not a big fan of roller coasters. I thought they were thrilling and a big rush, but by the time the coasters reached the top to take the first plunge, my heart would jump out of my chest, and I was always sorry that I had gone on the ride in the first place.

This day stands out above some of the rest because my mom made me an outfit to wear for the trip, which was gorgeous. I felt like a movie star that day. Sunglasses and all.

We were so poor when I was a kid that for most of my experience with school and my clothes, I took a lot of criticism. I would hear things in the hallway and in the girl's bathroom from some of the girls like, "Oh Sara, do you have another outfit on today that your mom made you from the rag bag collection? Poor Sara, she has no style."

Most of the girls at school bought their clothes at this little boutique in a nearby shopping center. It was not fashionable to make your own clothes. Handmade was not considered special, at least by the girls at my school. It meant that you were poor. I remember the brand name the girls threw around a lot was Bobbie Brooks. Everything matched. The sweaters, the skirts, the ribbons in their hair. Even their shoes. I knew the store well that the girls in my class all shopped at, but I had never been inside the store myself. We just did not have the money to buy anything, so I always felt like, why would I go in to just walk around the store if I could not afford to buy anything.

I had a job cleaning a beauty shop at the same shopping center after school that was a few doors down from the clothing store. I would walk past the boutique entrance really fast and look the other way. I did not want any of my classmates to see me walking by, and I also did not want them to know I was cleaning the beauty shop just a few doors down.

For mom being someone who had lost her real mother

when she was just a little girl and had a stepmother who treated her badly and who also taught her nothing, our mom had a lot of homemaking skills and special artistic talents. I think our mom was amazing.

Our mother could sew, knit, crochet, bake, cook, and she was a talented artist. She could draw freehand anything, artistically paint anything, and she would always have a beautiful, finished piece of art. Whatever it was, it was first place Blue Ribbon quality.

For my upcoming class trip, my mom took me shopping at the sewing store at the same shopping center. It was close to the beauty shop where I worked. Together we went there to pick out a pattern for an outfit of my choice. While inside the store, I was worried I would be spotted through the big glass windows by one of the girls from school. If so, I knew I would be talked about in the girl's bathroom at school the next day, that they had seen me shopping at the do-it-your-self sewing store.

The pattern books you looked through at the store were huge. It took a lot of time to look through them. If you did find something you liked, it listed a pattern number. Next, you went over to these big file drawers in the store and searched for your pattern packet which was filed in numerical order. Much to my surprise, mom and I found a two-piece outfit that we thought I would look awesome in. I was also surprised that my mom thought it was appropriate. Not because it was risqué but because it would show a little bit of my tummy. The pants had a cropped leg look, and the top was a sleeveless crop top. It showed just a little bit of my midriff. Just enough to feel innocently sexy. Something that Audrey Hepburn might wear. Next, we had to find the right material. We both gravitated to and picked out a lime green fabric with large fern leaves on it. What made this color and style extra special for me was I always sported a beautiful summer tan. This color looked beautiful when we held it up to my tanned arms and legs at the store. During the spring and summer, I worked in the fields with my dad, who farmed his mother's farm. Grandma Sara Ann lost her second husband, so my dad, who needed a job, started planting and harvesting soybeans. I hated working in the hot sun hoeing weeds, but if there was a plus, it did produce a nice farmer's tan for me. While inside the store, I went from feeling sorry for myself to feeling excited about how great this outfit was, and I could not wait to be able to show it off.

The outfit my mom made did turn out gorgeous. When it was finished, my mom had made it look like a professional designer had made it. For this class trip, this was one of the few days that I was not embarrassed or shy or feeling like I was not as cool as the other girls. This day at the amusement park, there were lots of people making eye contact and smiling at me. The girls from my class did not point at me and make fun. Although they also never complimented me either but they did stare at me and took notice. I watched their reactions. I imagined they were thinking that I looked great. I knew there was no way they would tell me. If any of them had asked me that day where did I buy my outfit, I would have proudly said, "My mother made this for me." I would have shouted it from the entertainment stage at the amusement park. I felt that special.

Our mom suffered from Alzheimer's in a nursing home for several years. Even when she had declined to where she did not recognize who I was anymore and would stare past me, I kept sharing with her about how amazing she was, how talented, how beautiful. I often talked to her about the special lime green outfit that she made for me, and I would ask her if she remembered. She never did, but I kept asking in the days, weeks, and years ahead. After all those years, I still very much wanted her to know what a huge impact that had on my life and my self-esteem. I wanted her to know she was amazing in so many ways. My mother, the little girl who lost her mother and had felt no love at all growing up, yet she accomplished so much. A successful career and personal life. A life that was hard for an exceptionally long time but eventually got better for her as she got older. She grew and blossomed as a person, a mother, and had a happy second marriage.

I thank God for the years she enjoyed life before Alzheimer's stole what was left. She made her life better through her faith in God and her strong and stubborn determination.

Years ago, my mom gave me a special handwritten note she called a Trust Document that reads, "I will always be there for you." We each shared this Trust Document with each other at church one Sunday. I keep this close to me. I find comfort in believing that she is watching over me and helping me through the hard parts of my life. I believe she is looking down over all her family, and she is hoping that we make the crooked parts straight and that we always do a good job.

Love you, Mom!

CHAPTER NINETEEN

KENTUCKY BLUEGRASS: NANCY

Nancy remembers looking out the car window in the back of the station wagon as her mom started making her way to their new home in Kentucky. As Evelyn drove a little further in what was known as a holler, the houses took on a whole new look. These were tiny little shacks. It went from bad to worse.

When the car stopped and they all got out, the reality of what this looked like was nothing short of being bad. Soon Nancy found out there were no indoor toilets or running water, and the heat was an old coal stove. It was so tiny and dirty. They would be living on top of each other. This was just another layer on top of her already horrible crappy life.

Living in Kentucky for Nancy was short-lived. As soon as they arrived and moved their things in, the abuse had started up again. Nancy ran away from home on her 16th birthday. She made her way back to her sister's apartment in Indiana. She could not take the abuse any longer.

When she arrived back in Indiana and started to get settled in, Nancy found out her high school sweetheart Lance was in town on leave from the Marine Corps. She was thrilled to hear this news. Enthusiastically she called Lance to make plans to get together. It was like they had never been apart. Both were happy and excited to be back together again. Nancy and Lance were very much in love with each other, and so they were married about two weeks later. Lance would be returning to his military base in Virginia, and this time, he would be taking his new bride with him.

For Nancy, the Marine Corps' life changed her life for the better. She absolutely loved everything about it. It offered structure and a family bond among all the families living on the base. Life there for her and Lance was an incredibly happy time for them both. The families living on the base became their new family. The families became close and shared meals and special times together.

Nancy volunteered for everything that was optioned for military wives to get involved with. She was extremely proud to be the wife of a marine and wanted to be a big part of military life.

She and Lance had a little baby girl in the first year that they were married. Lance came from a family of ten children, so he was excited about starting their family together.

Nancy loved being a mother and a wife. She remembered all the conversations she had with herself about wanting to be a wonderful wife and mother when she grew up. She made promises to be nothing like the home life she came from. She spoiled their precious little girl and made sure she knew how much she was loved. She packed Lance's lunch, cooked their dinner, and they genuinely loved each other. They never fought or argued about anything. Such a stark difference from her life as a child growing up. This all felt like a fairy tale. It was good to know that life could be good and wonderful after all.

One important thing that Lance encouraged Nancy to do was to go back to school to get her high school diploma. She agreed that she should, and she did. She said this achievement was one of the proudest accomplishments in her life. She wore her cap and gown and walked across that stage as proud as she could be. She said the only negative thing that she picked up while attending night school was that she started smoking pot with some of the other students.

While Lance was stationed in Japan, Nancy decided to take a full-time job working for a major chain store. She quickly worked her way up to management status and was managing several stores and employees and making incredibly good money. She was in her early thirties, so it felt good to be young and successful. Heban was wrong; she wasn't stupid. She was ambitious and smart.

At some point, while Lance was in Japan, he said he heard some rumors and suspected that Nancy was having an affair with someone she worked with. She was not having an affair. Although she was going out after work on occasion and enjoying herself.

Lance, in retaliation for what he thought was happening, foolishly had an affair. That was a deal-breaker for Nancy, and that ended their marriage. Nancy had and still does have an issue with trusting people. Because of her childhood, she has a lack of trust in anybody or anything. His having an affair was a deal-breaker for her. She had lost all trust in him, and she simply could not handle that. She was done, and there was nothing that could change her mind. She wanted a divorce.

Shortly after the decision to end her marriage, she became close with someone at work. She was his boss. Their relationship grew, and still today, they are together. She feels this special guy is her soul mate and they were destined and meant to be together.

But before making this life together with her soul mate permanent, Nancy had some low times in her life that she did not see coming.

Nancy never felt a close connection to God. Part of that was because she never had any religious exposure while growing up. Bible school one week in the summer was all she ever knew. With everything they lived through as kids, it was hard to believe in God anyway. She would ask herself, *What kind of God would allow this to happen to these innocent children?* She started thinking and felt that God did not love her, and she was not worthy of his love. She was damaged goods. She had heard that almost every day when she was a child.

One day she attended church with a friend. It felt meaningful and good, so she went back to the same church a few days later. She decided to be baptized, and it would take place in a public swimming pool. This new life with Christ for her only lasted about three weeks. She said she fell off the wagon, so to speak, and lost her faith in God. She went back to her old feelings of unworthiness and being damaged goods. No wonder she thought. I'm not surprised she thought, how could God possibly love her?

At one point over a three-month period, Nancy was doing cocaine. She wanted to feel better about herself and a lot of things, and she thought cocaine was the answer. She overdosed one night and came awfully close to dying. This really scared Nancy that she had come so close to death. She felt like she had fallen to the bottom of the barrel. She felt ashamed and unworthy. After all, she had just proved it to be true.

This near-death happening was her all-important wake-up call. Nancy said it felt like her soul was on fire and that demons had completely taken over.

The very next Sunday, Nancy decided to get up and go to church. That strong, determined little person inside of her was waking up and pushing her to get back on track. When she arrived at church that Sunday, she said it felt like the doors of the church opened just for her and said to her, "Come home, child." She immediately felt a sense of hope, love, and belonging.

That day in church, she sat in the pew, and when it was altar call, she knelt at the altar in the front of the church and asked God to please take all this pain and hurt away. She said God told her, "If you bring all your problems to me, I will take care of you." Nancy said she felt a lifting and truly felt a sense of relief. She felt different all over. Like all the bad and evil spirits had been washed away. She stayed there kneeling at the altar for a long time, and she was crying. She felt so unworthy of God's love, and she wanted to stay there until she felt his love and forgiveness. She said God spoke to her and said, "Welcome home, child."

Nancy shared that with her every breath in life today, she is better knowing that she is with God. After giving her life to Christ that Sunday morning, she went back to church that night. She went back on Wednesday for the prayer service, and she has faithfully continued to be faithful to God, attend church, and tries to live her life in a good way. She shared that she is never afraid to ask God for anything, and she feels he blesses her life every single day.

She knew, as a true Christian, there was one thing that she still had to do. She had to forgive Heban, her stepfather, for everything he had done. By this time, Heban was sick with bone cancer, and it had spread throughout his body. She felt forgiving him was also important to her mother. She did forgive Heban, but she will never be able to forget. Heban never said he was sorry for anything.

The special man in Nancy's life now is also a survivor of sexual and physical abuse. Together they have found strength and courage because of their strong Christian faith. Her life partner, when asked, will tell you that Nancy is the most amazing and strong person that he has ever known. With the Lord's blessing, they feel that together they can conquer and manage anything.

When Nancy's mother, Evelyn, died, in her will, she left everything to her son Jacob. The son she had with Heban. This was and still is very hurtful for Nancy, and it leaves her questioning why her mother did this. It is not because she had to be left anything big and significant by her mother. It has everything to do with not feeling loved enough by her mother to even be thought of. To at least be remembered and mentioned.

It is so hard for her to make any sense of her and her siblings' childhood. It was awful. It was criminal. It was a nightmare.

Nancy, for her life now and forevermore, says that God's promises and love shine brightly on her and over-shadows the darkness of her past.

CHAPTER TWENTY

KENTUCKY BLUEGRASS: KATIE

A short while after the family all moved without her to Kentucky, Katie went to visit her family. She could not believe how they were all living. She said that she would not have wished this life on a dog. There was no running water, a bucket left inside for a toilet. She said her sister Maria would have to go to the creek outside in the winter to wash her hair.

Sometimes the creek would flood, and since they lived at the top of the holler, they would be stranded there for days until the water level went back down.

Heban and Evelyn were able to somehow secure a loan from a local bank on the land because there was value in the land because of the coal. The land had never been stripped of the coal there. In this area of Kentucky, coal mining was the best job opportunity, and the land that had coal was most valuable. At some point, Katie thought that Heban might have started receiving social security disability because of his back issues.

Once they had their loan, they built a log cabin first for Heban's parents, and then Heban built a home for Evelyn and the kids.

Nancy was living with Katie while Lance was in Japan. Katie and Nancy planned a visit to Kentucky to visit their mother and siblings after they had completed building the houses and they were actually living in them. They were glad to see the living conditions had improved and were much better. After their visit, they both returned to Katie's apartment in Indiana.

Soon after Katie married her second husband, at some point, he went a little crazy and threatened to kill her. By this time, her mom and Heban were in their new house, so Katie called her mother and asked her if she could move to Kentucky and live with them temporarily. She was broke and desperate and had nowhere else to go. So, it truly was her only option and last resort. Why else would she move there? It was crazy to go there, but it was truly out of hopelessness and desperation.

When she moved, she was expected to get a job and help pay her way, and so she did. She did not have a problem with doing that. She was able to get a job paying $1.00 per hour. Not much, but it was a job.

While living in Kentucky, Katie met her third husband. They had a baby girl. Katie stayed married to this husband for seventeen-and-a-half years. He was a hard worker and a good husband and was loving and good to Katie. His only vice was he drank too much. But he always paid his bills first and took good care of his family before he ever spent any money on drinking.

He worked as a coal miner and had provided for them very well until he was hurt at work and could not work anymore. She had always wanted to be in the medical profession, so she decided to take classes, and she became certified as an EMT, Emergency Medical Technician. She even liked the sound of it. While her husband was sitting at home, unable to work and help pay the bills, he started getting jealous and accusing her of being unfaithful. This was causing a lot of problems and arguments, and they ended up getting a divorce.

Katie met her fourth husband after time went by. He happened at the time they met to be working for her sister Nancy at one of the chain stores she managed. He was much younger than Katie. He loved Katie very much, and he treated her like a queen. Of all her husbands, he was the most loving to her. Together they started working for a different company, and they worked the same shifts. Katie said one day they were standing at the time clock getting ready to punch in when her husband had a fatal heart attack at age thirty-seven and fell to the floor. Katie tried using CPR on him as she was trained to do, but there was nothing she could do. He was gone. This was an awfully hard time for Katie, and her sisters were great support for her. They were there for her day and night.

When it came to believing in God, Katie had not had much exposure to church, God, and the Bible. At the time that her husband died, her mom and Heban had joined a church, and they were attending every Sunday. Heban, the devil himself, was now going to church. Katie went a few times with them, and it felt good, she said, to hear about God's love. So, Katie set about to try and attend a few different churches trying to find one that she really felt she wanted to be a part of.

Katie finally found a church that she liked the preacher and his sermons. She felt she connected with him and what he preached. She felt stronger spiritually and more peaceful. To this day, she has stayed with this same pastor and church.

Katie now has health issues, stage four COPD, and is

on oxygen. She is not able to make the church services but can watch the sermons live on her TV. Her health keeps her home most of the time these days.

For all the years of abuse and not feeling loved, Katie shared that having a close and loving relationship with God pulls her through whatever life brings. She feels if God called her home today, she is ready. She said God had spared her life many times when she thought her life was over. When she thought she would not survive the beatings or the times she tried to commit suicide. She praises God for everything in her life.

As a kid and being beaten every day, she feels God brought her through it every time. She did not know God back then, but she always felt there was something there. Someone or something that she could not see. Someone watching over her. There was a reason she was not dead. God has blessed her with two wonderful children and grand and great-grandchildren too.

She is so grateful for her siblings and all that they have survived. She is proud of them as she says they have got their acts together. After all that they had been through as children, it is amazing and good where all of them are now, even though the pain and heartbreak are still with all of them.

Katie said she does not care that Heban suffered before he died because so many times, she had wished for him to die. She wanted him dead. She was there for her mom during this time because, for whatever reason, she said her mom really loved Heban. Katie said it might not sound like a Christian for her not feeling bad for Heban and his pain, but it is honest, and it is how she feels.

She used this phrase a lot when we talked together, "Damned if you do, and you are damned if you do not."

After Heban died, her mom and Jacob got even closer. Her mom allowed Jacob to take over and be her boss.

After Heban died, her mother finally admitted to knowing some of what had been going on. Her mother's why for all the kids is still not clear, or even how she could have let all the abuse happen to her children and herself. Katie knows Heban threatened her and all of them. But still, she said it just feels that there had to be a better way. She said, we are all mothers ourselves, and we do not see any of us making that same choice and allowing our children to suffer like that.

Her mother and her siblings all became closer after

Heban died. They had about eleven good years with their mother after he passed. They could visit without fear and retaliation. Their Mom left this world and left all that she had in worldly possessions to her son Jacob. Katie speculated that maybe Heban made her promise to do that, or maybe that is what she wanted.

Katie does not want to dwell on what her mother's reasons for any of this might be. Katie is at peace with herself, knowing that she is a better mother and grandmother for all of this. And she likes who she is.

The words she wants to leave with everyone are: "Never give up hope, even in your darkest hours." "Keep hoping and praying and believing forever and always."

CHAPTER TWENTY-ONE

DANIEL IS IN TOWN

I graduated from high school in May of 1969. It was a year that marked a lot of radical changes. Our era was the peace and love generation. The Flower children were trying to affect change. Nineteen sixty-nine has been called one of the most culturally defining years to date. On August 15, 1969, in Bethel, New York, a landmark was born that is still talked about today. Legendary performers played to a crowd of over 450,000 people at the Woodstock Music Festival. The pictures and stories surrounding these three legendary days made a forever impression on the heartbeat and new direction of our country.

Hippie members were calling and pushing for a spiritual revolution, a return to faith, and a lifestyle of the early Christians. Young people questioned and did not approve of America's materialism, culture, and political beliefs. This was not really anything new or something that had not happened before, except at this time in history, they pushed harder at every level to affect change. This was called the counterculture. We had alternative lifestyles, radical lyrics in songs, billboards, signs, sit-ins, protests, females burning their bras, and other radical rantings.

The clothing style that was in were bell-bottom pants, maxi dresses, ponchos, and frayed out jeans. This was a continuation of the hippie style of the 1960s.

In both the 1960s and 1970s, we were surrounded by what was called then "Free Love." This sexually active life-style with casual sex partners really whittled away at our beliefs of the church about commitment and our wedding vows of death till we part. It became difficult to trust your partner when it came to staying faithful to each other because it seemed that it was being widely common and cool to be unfaithful. This Free Love era caused an even further gap between the teachings and beliefs of the church and God's Word.

Music was played from eight-track tapes from artists like Donna Summer and Marvin Gaye. Rock bands that were taking the stage were groups like Queen, Rolling Stones, and Pink Floyd. Names we still hear and listen to today. Then came Disco. Disco was a whole new beat and sound, and disco dancing became all the rage. Disco dance clubs started popping up everywhere.

Churches, however, began seeing drops in their membership and attendance. It had actually started in the 1950s after World War II, but with the war in Vietnam, church leaders became more vocal about America's involvement. A lot of churches opposed the war. The women's movement also affected church participation. The birth control pill and attitudes about sex greatly affected the Catholic church. The Evangelical movement started to gain popularity along with the birth of televangelism.

My mother, for the first time, was on her own after my father died in August 1970. She had two teenage children, my brother and sister, to finish raising. I was already married and out of the house.

My mom had a good job, and for the very first time in her life, she felt like a whole new world awaited her. One where she was allowed to have fun and have girlfriends, buy some new clothes, and maybe later meet a nice man, maybe go out to dinner together, or maybe even take a few nice trips.

She wanted to buy herself some new clothes and shoes and get her hair done. Because mom had married at age sixteen, she went from living at home with her dad and stepmother to being a wife and having a husband who ruled and made all the decisions. But now she was single, and she was her own boss, with two capable teenage children. She was living at a time where the world around her was filled with new opportunities for women. A time for her to explore her passions. To find out who she was as a person, as a woman, but still very much a mother. She was still young. She was just thirty-eight years old.

Mom became active in many different things. She was voted in as a board member for a few different lending institutions and businesses. She also became active in numerous club opportunities and started achieving special recognitions and awards. She was finding and using talents that she really did not know she had. People thought she was smart, attractive and many people liked her.

She took up bowling and joined a few leagues, and she was an excellent and extremely competitive bowler. She had found her voice. She had found passion in living life. She had not been excited about having fun for herself for such a long time. The last time she felt this much enthusiasm dated back to when she was a cheerleader in high school.

Through one of her girlfriends at work, mom met a guy named Jack. He had lost his wife and was just starting to date. Mom shared with me that she really liked Jack, and they were having a lot of fun. Mom really fell hard for him, and she was not keeping it a secret that she was hoping they would end up being together long-term. Possibly marriage. They did date for almost a year when for some reason, Jack wanted to break things off. My mother was devasted and had not seen it coming. She took it hard because she immediately fell back into the old feelings as a young girl of not being pretty enough or smart enough. She felt she just did not measure up. It broke my heart to see my mom hurt like this.

Mom had a couple of fun-loving girlfriends who were single, and they swooped in to rescue her. They assured her that it was his loss, and she could do better anyways. Together the gals planned and made a few island trips. From the stories they told, they had a lot of laughs and met some nice men.

She changed jobs at some point and was doing extremely well within this company. She was moving up in position and pay. She did administration and secretarial work for several engineers within the company. She was well thought of by the engineers and respected. She had an excellent work ethic.

Soon my brother announced that he was getting married and he would be moving out of the house. My younger sister was dating, and about a year later, she announced she was planning on getting married too. My sister had already moved out into her own apartment before getting married.

Sometime during the year 1975, Mom received a phone call from a voice from the past. It was that younger brother of her best girlfriend in high school, Daniel. The pesty little kid that had a crush on her and was always trying to show off to impress her. Daniel told her that he was in town visiting his younger brother, and he would like to see her for old times' sake and take her out for dinner. He went on to tell her that he had been living in southern Ohio and had married and had an adopted son, but that he had just recently divorced and was planning to move back to the small town he grew up in. This way, he would be closer to his mother and siblings. His father had passed away a few years before.

Mom had not seen him since she was in high school, and so she was a little curious. Her initial thoughts were that he was quite a bit younger than her, but it did not have to be an actual date. It could be a time to just catch up and to talk about old times. She was thirty-nine, and he was thirty-two. Seven years difference was a bigger gap when she was a teenager at age fifteen, and he was only eight years old at the time. At eight years old, he was just an annoying little boy. She thought maybe at age thirty-two, it would not feel like such a big age gap. Also, she was hoping he would be less annoying at this age.

Daniel told her that he had been in the navy. Dating a guy that had been in the service and served his country was appealing to her. He also said he was in sales, selling major appliances, and had won awards each year as a top producer. So far, it all sounded promising. She was hoping he had a full head of hair, a great smile, and was kind. She called me to let me know about his call. I was sitting on pins and needles waiting to hear about their first date remembering the heartbreak she had after the break-up with the last guy.

The first date was amazing for both. They laughed and reminisced and made plans for another date. Their dates kept happening, and one day after only a few months, they decided they wanted to set a date to get married. Daniel and Elizabeth were married in 1976. By this time, my mother had grandchildren with more on the way. Daniel was excited about becoming a grandfather and offering any fatherly advice if wanted. Daniel and Elizabeth absolutely adored all the special get-togethers and special family time.

Daniels's son had been adopted and still lived with his

mother. However, he did come to visit his dad often. Unfortunately, shortly after they married, his son caused some financial and legal issues for them, and it was hard to trust him at times. Eventually, he left town and hid his whereabouts for whatever reasons. The rest of the family could only speculate that it may have been drugs. It was heartbreaking for Daniel and my mom because they really wanted the best for him and had high hopes for his future.

Their years of marriage together brought with it years of fun, travel, and new friends. They had snowmobiles, a motor home, a big house they remodeled. They lived life in a big way, making fun their focus.

The biggest negative that anyone could call attention to about Daniel was all the money-making ideas he had. He was always so passionate about his business ventures. Everyone always wished them the best. But some of the business ideas and ventures took a big bite out of their retirement monies which later in their lives would prove to cause a financially hard time for them. But still, despite it all, they enjoyed many fun-loving years of being together.

CHAPTER TWENTY-TWO

THE STEPMOTHER STORY

On a rare occasion of even seeing and talking to my mother's stepmother, she shared with me an update about my cousins. The story she told me about my cousins and my aunt moving to Kentucky sounded glamorous to me. It sounded like they had struck it rich because they were going to make a big killing off all the coal on the property they owned. Good for them. For others, their riches might have come from a gold mine or diamonds. But coal was a big and important commodity too. So, I was genuinely happy for them even though I did not really know them. At least things turned out good for them. It was 1973, and I was twenty-two years old when they moved to Kentucky as land barons. I had not seen any of them since they were all little. It was incredibly good to think and hear that everything was wonderful for them.

In 1973 the United States troops withdrew from Vietnam, and the US involvement in the Vietnam War ended. I had several friends who had been drafted right out of high school, and some of them would not be coming home. Those that did make it back were not the same person. The war had stolen their youth and replaced it with PTSD, addictions, and nightmares. Some had lost body parts too. It was heartbreaking to see, especially for these young men, because they were not celebrated and thanked for their service to our country. What kind of country do we live in where we celebrate more our celebrities, athletes, and politicians over our heroes who care for us, protect us, and fight for our freedom?

I also have strong feelings about our country and our religious freedoms being protected. About having love and respect for each other. Having fame and fortune is not a bad thing at all, and I am happy for others, but it is what you do with that gift that matters. Our first responders, our military, our doctors, nurses are so important. For without them, we are sick, and we live our lives in danger.

I only remember my aunt Evelyn and her husband Heban and their little boy Jacob coming to visit once when Jacob was about five years old. He wore a gun and holster on his hip as he hopped around our kitchen and dining room and pretended to shoot us with his toy gun. He was chubby and loud but at the same time still cute. I was not sure about the rest of the kids, my cousins, and I never asked about them either. I am not sure why. I would guess because, at the time, I was still a kid myself, maybe about sixteen years old. I am sure I assumed they were all okay, or my aunt would have told us if there were any problems. I really do not remember what the visit was for. Only that it was rare that she came to our house, and I think, honestly, it might have been the only visit ever while my aunt was married to Heban. On this day, she had come to see my mom. My mom seemed to be happy to see her.

As a kid growing up, I never knew about the beatings and sexual abuse my cousins suffered. As far as I knew, they were privileged kids. My grandmother Mildred wanted me to think I was not as lucky as they were, my cousins. But for me, I was never the kind of child then or kind of person now that resented what someone else has. It was okay by me.

What I thought I knew from the stories about my aunt was that she had married some tycoon guy who bought this big place for all of them to live, and it was in Indiana. He was a truck driver that also owned a big fleet of trucks. This turned out not to be true. He did not own a fleet, but he was a truck driver.

Indiana sounded like quite a large investment opportunity with a motel, restaurant, service station, and a big house. He had to be rich. It sounded like after seven years living in Indiana and successfully running that business, they sold it, and then this very smart and successful businessman, Heban, saw a bigger and better opportunity. He was now a land baron high in the mountains of Kentucky and was moving all the family there. My aunt and her children must for sure be living a dream come true.

I had visions of Kentucky bluegrass, the Kentucky Derby, mint juleps. Galloping horses in the pasture, sunsets behind the mountain range. In my world, and according to my grandma Mildred, my mother's stepmother, my aunt Evelyn had picked herself a real winner in choosing her second husband, Heban. Mildred said he was nothing like that drunk she married the first time. She went on to say, "Any man willing to take on five of her children had to be a saint."

So, my version about their lives off the lips of my mother's stepmother Mildred told a much different story. I would learn little by little about the horrors they suffered in bits and tiny pieces over the next several years.

Why my mother's stepmother and father wanted to

keep us all apart and then not be truthful about each other's lives is lost in a sea of not understanding why. Why they wanted to keep the sisters apart and always instigating untrue stories to stir trouble between them is lost in that same sea of not knowing why and understanding.

It all just seems so dysfunctional and complicated, and it makes you wonder, for what purpose.

All this just wasted the possibility for all of us of having each other to know and grow with. To support each other, to be there for each other. I know throughout many days in my life, when I was going through something hard, if I had known then that I had a cousin who would pray for me and was genuine about my concerns, this would have helped to get me through. We have that for each other now, and it is amazing and wonderful. For all the times, my cousins were desperate and feeling hopeless because no one was there for them, and no one believed them. If I would have known and we would have been in touch and connected with each other, I could have been a lifeline for them. When I was married and out of the house, I could have offered safety and refuge. Like the story from the Diary of Anne Frank, I would have hidden them away and helped to protect them. They were afraid and desperate.

My cousins told me that their grandmother Mildred had told them that their aunt Elizabeth's children were not their real cousins and that we did not want anything to do with them.

It was a step of courage for Nancy to track me down shortly before my mother passed away. She was not sure if I would want to meet, but she wanted at least to see my mom before she passed. It was this important phone call that put some light on the years of lies and stories we all had been hiding and told. It was this important first step that put us on the path we are on now.

A time for healing and time for sharing our life stories in hopes that someone else that is hurting and feeling hopeless who may be going through some of the same hurts and abuses will know and find comfort that "This too shall pass." God is here, He loves you, and He sees your suffering. Have faith and keep praying. You can make it to the other side. There is hope in these pages for you.

CHAPTER TWENTY-THREE

MARIA'S PASSION

Maria said one of her mother's favorite sayings was, "Dynamite comes in small packages." Maria gained strength and courage as she grew up because she had to. Her sister Nancy had coached her on developing her survival skills. As Maria grew, she became a strong-willed and strong-minded person. Her fear of water and wanting to shield herself from hearing bad news on TV is not to be mistaken that she was weak, afraid, or cowardly. If you push Maria too far, she will dig her heels in and take a firm stand, and there is no backing down.

Maria has a huge trust issue. This is true for all her siblings, and it is very understandable. Their entire childhood was filled with lies, deception, and abuse. Maria also has a big issue with people that blame their childhood lives for everything that goes wrong in their life. Blaming their childhood for why they turned to a life of crime, addictions, or living a life of nothingness. It is my sister's fault she ruined my life. I was never treated fairly. They loved you more. I was so abused. Maria wants to stand on the rooftops and shout out to everyone to hear that life is what you make of it and do not let your past rule your future.

Maria's bond with her siblings is her biggest strength. That is not to say they do not have disagreements because they do. Maria said, "I can be as mad as a wet hen sometimes, but that soon passes, I deeply love them, and I am proud of each of them too."

Growing up, if one child had to go to bed hungry, they all stuck together, and they all went to bed hungry. They took beatings for each other. That commitment and bond remains strong today.

Maria's walk with God happened when she was seventeen years old. Her mother, Evelyn, and her mother's father, and stepmother, Maria's grandparents, were baptized by the preacher from their church. The baptism was in the creek that was nearby to their house. Maria stood back a safe distance on the bank of the creek and watched. On the following Saturday night, there was a big revival, and the preacher showed a film about hell. After the film was over, the preacher said, "I have been teaching you all about heaven, but tonight we are learning about hell. Somebody here and I do not know who you are, wants to be saved." Maria felt like he was looking directly at her. She had a friend sitting next to her. The preacher then said, "Bow your heads.

I'm just going to come to you if you just raise your hand. I won't point you out." Maria was not able to raise her hand for some reason, and instead, she raised her head and looked up at him. This was in the month of February, and it was cold outside. Maria was going to be baptized in the freezing cold water in the creek while nervously remembering that she was scared to death of water. Maria had two people holding her up, and she begged them to please not let go of her.

Maria has never smoked. She does not drink, and she does not use foul language. She admits that at times she does have thoughts that she feels bad about. She knows God would not want her to say and think this way. When times like that happen, she prays on it. Maria takes herself back to the day that she was baptized at seventeen years old, and she gave her life to the lord. Maria always dreamed, hoped, and prayed for a better life. She wanted more out of her life than her real father and mother ever had.

Life for Maria after the move to Kentucky was just as bad as it was in Indiana. Maria was a sophomore in high school when they moved there. Living in the mountains and hills of Kentucky was a big culture shock. Living in the holler with no running water, outhouses, and no electricity. To go to school and to catch the school bus meant you had to walk about a mile down to the bottom of the holler to catch the bus. Muddy, wet, and a lot of times dark in the morning.

Maria has always had a passion for saving people. Her biggest hope was to one day be a flight nurse. Maria wanted to work in trauma settings where people were in life-or-death situations. She wanted to be one of the best at her job and save people's lives. Maria knew this passion and deep desire came from her own life. She always felt desperate and afraid growing up. She always hoped someone would walk through the door and save her and save her mother and siblings. Maria cried and begged for this to happen, but no one ever came. That feeling of hopelessness and desperation haunted her. So, it became her passion to save others. To come to their rescue.

CHAPTER TWENTY-FOUR

CYNTHIA HELPS A FRIEND

Cynthia believes that worry is God's way to grow our faith.

Cynthia had been holding on to hope that the move to Kentucky would mean a fresh start and maybe a better life. The first clue that told her that was not going to be the case was the desolate one-lane dirt path they turned on. It was not a road. The drive on the path going up to the holler was overgrown, dark, eerie, and secluded. It was so desolate and uncivilized that Cynthia started to think that they were all going to die there. That this was Heban's plan all along. He was finally going to kill them, and no one would ever know. When the car finally stopped, Cynthia looked out and said, "Where is our house?" Someone pointed to this small metal building, and Cynthia's jaw dropped. She was in disbelief. She thought that the building was a storage shed to store the lawnmower. This could not actually be where they were going to live. Cynthia was shocked and about to cry. She did not think things could be any worse than what they had left in Indiana, but this was by far a whole lot worse.

Five children and four adults all crowded together inside this metal shed with no running water and no electricity. The beds were homemade rustic bunk beds that Heban and Max built. It was decided that Cynthia would be on the top bunk with her sister Maria. There was hardly enough room on the top bunk for one person to sleep. This was going to be hard.

Max had been working on bringing logs down from the mountain to build a house before all the family arrived. The first log cabin being built would be for Heban's parents. Now that the girls had arrived, they would have to start helping with this work too.

Soon the kids and Evelyn realized that they had escaped nothing after leaving Indiana. The physical and sexual abuse was happening here too.

There was a creek that ran along the side of the path of the holler. About three miles away, the creek widened. This is where people went swimming. Neither Cynthia nor Maria ever went swimming because of their fear of water. But both still enjoyed going. They would sit on the bank and watch all the other kids. One day when they were sitting on the bank, a boy came over and sat next to Maria. He sat there for a while, and then he leaned over and gave Maria a kiss. Maria did not know him, and his kiss was completely unexpected. Unfortunately, it had to be a day that Heban had driven to the swimming hole to pick the kids up. Heban saw the boy kiss Maria. On this day, Heban was in a worse mood than usual because he was out of his narcotics. His rage was always worse when he did not have his drugs. In the car on the ride home, the fear everyone felt was all-consuming. They knew this was going to turn out bad for Maria. After everyone got out of the car and inside the house, Heban grabbed Maria and gave her a beating for letting the boy kiss her. Heban did not allow her to tell him that she did not even know him, and she did not know he was going to kiss her. He did not care. Then Heban grabbed Evelyn and beat her for having a daughter that would let a boy kiss her like that.

Cynthia and her siblings still had to spend time in the bedroom with Heban to be able to go to school functions. Heban almost always would follow them wherever they were going and watch their every move.

For the girls, if Heban saw you sitting and talking with any boys, that was going to be guaranteed big trouble for you when you got home. One day Heban was busy working on something, so that day, he was not able to spy on Cynthia. Cynthia attended a ball game, and after the game, some friends brought her home. They wanted to come in and meet her parents, and Cynthia thought it might be okay to at least come inside and meet her mom. For whatever reason, this was not okay with Heban. He did not want anyone in his house. After her friends left, Heban flew into a rage. Heban whipped her so hard that she could not take a seat on the school bus the next morning. The bus driver reported that something was wrong with her, and she was sent to the guidance counselor. When the counselor asked her, what happened, she said that she fell down the steps at home. The counselor sent her to see the school nurse. The nurse checked Cynthia and concluded that it looked more like she had been beaten. This was not an accident. This was abuse. The school then called social services to report it. Next, the school called her mom and Heban and told them they needed to pick Cynthia up and that someone from social services would be coming to their house to talk with them.

Both her mom and Heban threatened Cynthia and told her that she had better tell the social worker that she fell down the stairs. Cynthia promised them that she would. The social worker arrived at their house about 6:00 p.m.

that night. Cynthia did as she said she would. She told the social worker that she fell on the stairs. There were no further questions, and the case was closed.

How many times do cases like this slip through the system, and the child remains in the home and continues to be abused? How many times is a child threatened and told to lie? How many children feel helpless, without any protection, and with no way to try and escape the abuse?

Going to church in Kentucky turned out to be a total family happening. Heban had family that had lived in this area for years, and they attended a nearby Baptist church. Being involved in the church was an important part of life for most families that lived in the hills of Kentucky. Heban, Evelyn, and the kids all started attending the same Baptist church. Cynthia and her siblings were not allowed to talk to anybody at church besides saying hello, goodbye, and thank you for fear that somebody might find out what was really going on behind closed doors. At church, in front of all the worshipers, Heban and Evelyn and the whole family were seen as just one big happy family. Heban sang hymns along with everyone else while raising his hands in the air and shouting out praises.

At about age seventeen, Cynthia met a boy, and she

very much wanted him to be her boyfriend. She approached this subject at home with Heban and her mom. It was decided that if this boy came to the house and did work that Heban wanted to be done, then Cynthia would be allowed to have him as her boyfriend. On Saturday mornings, her boyfriend would show up at 6:00 a.m., ready to be put to work. His name was James, and he would do anything and everything Heban asked him to do. He really liked Cynthia, so he was willing to work hard to please her stepfather. As time went on, Cynthia and James were getting more serious about each other.

Cynthia was a song leader at church, and one day, she suddenly passed out. This was a big scare for Cynthia, and she cried in the car all the way home. Her mother, Evelyn, called her dad, Henry, and her stepmother Mildred, Cynthia's grandparents, and asked them to come over to the house. By this time, her grandparents had moved and now lived close by to all of them in the holler. When her grandparents arrived, they all sat down at the table over coffee to talk. There was some small talk, and then Cynthia was asked if she was pregnant. Cynthia immediately became more upset and shouted out, "You all just leave me alone." She got up from the table and went to her bedroom, and slammed the door shut behind her. The next thing she knew, Heban pushed open the door and charged straight at her. He grabbed her by her hair and dragged her back to the table, and then smacked her hard in the face. Her grandmother then said, "You listen here. You kids had disgraced your mother and dad's name enough already when you lived in Indiana. They will not be disgraced by you again." Cynthia could not believe what she had just heard. All these thoughts started racing through her mind. She thought this was all so unbelievable. The parents are innocent, and the children are the bad ones. How does this even begin to make sense or even happen?

The next words coming out of Heban's mouth were, "You are either going to a home to have this baby, or I am going to stomp it out of you. Cynthia was shaking by now, and Evelyn told Cynthia that she would leave and go with her. When Heban heard this, he looked directly at Evelyn and said, "If you go with her, you will never see our son Jacob ever again. You need to tell her to get an abortion."

Cynthia's boyfriend James rode the same school bus as Cynthia did. When he did not see her on the bus that day, he called the house to make sure everything was okay. The rule at the house was that none of the kids were ever allowed to answer the phone. Heban answered the phone, and

James said hello and asked to speak to Cynthia. Heban told James that he and Evelyn were driving over to his house to talk to him. When they got to James' house and confronted him about getting Cynthia pregnant, James told them that he was not the father. James was scared to death of Heban, and he later told Cynthia that he felt his life was in danger.

When Evelyn and Heban returned home, they told Cynthia that she was kicked out of the house and she needed to go somewhere else to live. Heban feared that if this baby was not James' baby, there was a possibility that he was the father. He wanted her to disappear, and he did not care where.

Cynthia went to her room and packed her things and started walking down the holler. As she was walking along carrying her bag, a relative of Heban's stopped her and asked her where she was going. Heban's cousin and his wife were good people. They took Cynthia in for about three weeks. They never told anyone she was staying there. They never told anyone at church, nor their neighbors; no one ever knew. After three weeks there, Cynthia went to live with her sister Maria who was married and had a house with her husband.

One day Evelyn called James and told him to pick up

Cynthia at her sister Maria's house. Evelyn had money for him to purchase a bus ticket for Cynthia. Evelyn had decided for Cynthia that she needed to go and live with her sister Nancy who still lived in Indiana.

At Christmas time that same year, Nancy went to Kentucky to see her mom and siblings for the holidays. Cynthia was forbidden to come home. It was made known very loud and clear that she was not welcome in or near the house anymore.

Cynthia was encouraged by her mother to give the baby up for adoption. Cynthia reluctantly agreed and signed the papers to do so. The papers that she signed with the adoption service stated that her due date was April 7 and that she agreed to give up her full-term baby for adoption. Cynthia's son came early, and her beautiful, healthy boy was born on March 15. He was not a full-term baby, so legally, she was able to keep her precious little baby boy. The adoption service did not want a baby if it was not full term. Cynthia has always felt that God was at work in all of this. Cynthia never wanted to lose her baby or give him up, and James was the father.

After the baby was a few weeks old, she flew back to Kentucky. She wanted to see her mom. She never told them she was coming, and when she walked in with the baby, their heads dropped. They were not happy to see her. Her family was upset, and the tension was awful. Cynthia only stayed a few weeks because there was another big blow up and she did not feel safe for herself and her baby staying there.

Cynthia packed up and left. She was going to stay with some friends from church. As it had been before, these friends also kept it quiet about her staying with them. Nobody ever wanted to go up against Heban.

Cynthia married and then divorced and moved to Florida. After she had lived there for about two months, she was not feeling happy and decided she wanted to move back to Kentucky. She needed money to make the trip. She knew she had a brand-new radar detector that she had bought, so she decided to return it to the store to get some cash. She made the trip back to Kentucky.

Cynthia was baptized and saved when she was fifteen. But as time went on, she felt as though it had washed off, and she needed to try again. It was after moving back from Florida that she felt more strongly about this. This was a huge embarrassment to Heban. He claimed that she was making a fool out of him by getting baptized twice. But

Cynthia felt strongly about this. Heban asked her if she reckoned she would get it right this time. Cynthia tried to explain to him that the last time she was younger. That at the time, she was worried if she did not get baptized with the rest of her family when they died, they would all be in heaven. She would not have made it to heaven to be with them because she would not have been saved. For this next time of getting baptized, Cynthia wanted her mom to go with her to church, but Heban absolutely forbid it.

She had been praying for many years. Prayers like, "Please, dear God, don't let Heban drag me out of bed at night and beat me." She even took a red crayon and colored with it above the top of her bedroom door to help keep Heban out. She read in the Bible that the blood of Jesus would protect you.

Cynthia said life was hard for her being the youngest. When all her siblings had moved out, she was the only one left to suffer all the abuse. Her younger half-brother Jacob was never abused the way the other kids were.

Cynthia thought a lot about suicide at a lot of different times. What always stopped her from following through was not the fear of dying. She worried more about how it would be seen through the eyes of God. Cynthia knew the chapters and verses in the Bible, and the Bible said it was wrong to take your own life.

Cynthia, like her sister Maria, shared that she cannot watch a movie with violence; she must hide her face and cover her ears.

When Heban lay dying in bed, Cynthia told him she forgave him. He never asked for it, but she felt it was the right thing for her to do. She prayed that God would have mercy on his soul. Heban never ever said he was sorry for anything before he died.

After Heban died, there was a great relief for everyone in the family. Evelyn was, however, sad about his death. This is confusing and hard to understand after all she suffered and her kids suffered. What we did not know is that Jacob knew more than we thought. He said he hated what his dad did to his mother and his siblings. He said he sometimes saw things from outside and looking through the window. Jacob wondered why he never suffered the abuse that the rest of them all had. It makes you wonder if Heban could feel love. If so, maybe he loved Jacob. If he could love, he must have hated his stepchildren.

When each of the siblings started sitting down to tell their own stories, and privately, it was then that they found a lifting and a healing starting to take place in their spirits and lives. Before this, they could not talk openly even to each other about the abuse. It was too painful. They did not want to. They wanted those memories buried. All five of them suffer from PTSD.

Each of them has expressed that after sharing their stories, they had feelings of healing and great relief. They wanted their story to be told.

Their hope is that their life stories will help someone else who is suffering abuse. It will help others to know and have faith that they have a better future waiting for them. To say to others, stay strong, pray, and survive whatever you might be going through.

To be able to speak out loud about all of this brings deep pain but with it a huge sense of relief. No one ever believed them, and no one cared enough to save them. Words cannot express the fear and desperation they had every day of their life growing up.

This is their healing. This is their life story.

After Heban's passing, Evelyn and her children all grew closer. About eleven years after Heban died, Evelyn died after having a complicated surgery. When Cynthia lost her mother, she sank into a deep depression. She started attending therapy sessions because she was in a very dark place. She had lost the will to live. This is when she was first diagnosed with PTSD. Post Traumatic Stress Syndrome. This disorder is well known and common with people who have been in combat. Cynthia, just like her siblings, fought for her survival every day.

Cynthia is unable to keep her hands and feet from shaking, and she scares easily. She knows her greatest strength comes from God, so on her awfully bad days, she prays extra hard, and God helps to pull her through whatever it is.

Recently, Cynthia had a friend reach out to her and asked her to visit her. Her friend seemed depressed, and Cynthia thought her friend might tell her that she was sick with something bad. Her friend shared that she had been molested as a child, and she was having a hard time dealing with it. Cynthia felt that God had told her friend to contact her because she could be of help to her. Cynthia shared with her friend that she, too, had been abused and how she was dealing with it. She told her friend that healing begins when you can talk out loud. You do not have to hide and suffer alone anymore. It is not your fault.

CHAPTER TWENTY-FIVE

MAX LEAVES HOME

Heban, along with his mother, father, and Max, made the trip from Indiana to their new home in Kentucky. They went ahead of everyone else to get things ready before the rest of the family made the move. When Heban turned off the road, he started driving up a dirt path. It did not look like a road or even a path that had been traveled on. It had a creek that ran along the side of the path. He kept his mouth shut, but he was worried about where Heban was taking him. Max soon learned this was called the holler.

In Kentucky, a holler is a flat spot, a valley flat spot in the mountains. It lies between two sides of the mountains. It has been told by some that the name came about because if you lived on the opposite side of the mountain, you could holler to your friend on the other side. Each could holler back and forth because your voice would echo and carry.

When they reached the top of the holler and turned the motor off, much to Max's surprise, there was no house in front of them. He looked far and wide, and all he could see were trees and more trees. Afraid to ask questions, Max waited to be told what the plan was. Max did see an 8x10 metal building but thought that was for storage. Unfortunately, Heban told him the 8x10 metal building was their new home. There was no electricity, no running water, no heat. This was in the middle of nowhere. Max was scared that he might not ever make it out of there alive. All sorts of thoughts were running through his mind. He thought this could not possibly be where they were going to live. He suspected something else was up. It was hard to go to sleep that night.

They all slept on the floor of the building the night they arrived, and the next morning, Heban and Max started cutting trees to make beds for the entire family. They had no tables, no chairs, and no kitchen. A small add-on was made to the metal building to increase the living space. The second night in Kentucky, Max had a hard time sleeping too. The wild animal sounds were deafening, and they sounded and echoed like they were right outside the door. This was his new life in the mountains of Kentucky, and he did not much like it.

Sometime after they finished the add-on to the metal building and the beds were built, Heban said it was time to get Evelyn, Jacob, and the girls. They traveled back to pick them all up. When they all arrived at their new home in Kentucky, the look on all their faces was one of total shock and disbelief.

Life here would be totally different than living in Indiana. Heban bought an old workhorse for a good price and a plow. The entire family was going to become farmers. Max had to learn how to plow with the stubborn old workhorse. The first thing Max needed to learn was how to control the horse. He had never been around any horse before this. This was difficult for Max because he was not that strong yet. The horse was taking over control. Heban threatened Max that he had better learn fast and get it right, or he could just stay out there all night until he did. Along with the planting of the crops, Heban also bought a cow, some chickens, and two hogs. The one thing that Max did get good at was milking the cow without getting bucked.

Heban wanted to get started on building a log cabin, and Max had to help. Their land had plenty of trees on it, so a log cabin was a good choice. Max had no idea how to build a log cabin, but whether he wanted to or not, he was about to learn, and the first thing he learned was how to use a hand saw.

The area for the cabin needed to be cleared. This was a

lot of hard physical work, and it took a long time. Max had to get up early and start working, and he worked until after dark. Once the land was cleared, they were ready to start the cabin. The first cabin would be Heban's parents' home.

To build a log cabin, you first had to choose the best trees to cut down using your axe. Yes, this was Paul Bunyan-style, back-breaking work. There were no power tools. You went deep into the forest, looking and identifying the kind of tree you wanted for the cabin. White and red pine trees Max had been told, was a good option. That is because pine trees are good insulators from the cold. As it turned out, they used poplar trees because their land was most plentiful with poplars.

The old workhorse was used to hook up the logs to get them down the mountain. As the horse would start down the mountain, he would begin to pick up speed, and then the logs started dropping off. After the logs let loose and were falling, the horse would just take off, galloping away. Because Max was still young and not a big guy, he had a hard time controlling the horse. The horse was also smart and would remember the path so the horse would just take off because he knew where he was going. It was extremely hard to manage it all, no matter how hard Max tried. Sadly, this meant for Max that he was in trouble with Heban. Max was beaten many times for being weak, worthless, and unable to control the horse.

Deciding on the size of the cabin determined the number of logs that would be needed. The logs would have to be slash scored. Slash scoring is making a certain amount of axe cuts down the length of the log. Anyone who ever played with Lincoln logs would know that the notches in those toy logs allowed you to securely place and fit together the next log on top of it.

The three steps that had to be done were scoring, juggling, and hewing. Hewing is the process of converting the round log so that you have a flat surface. This was needed for stacking. This method for building a log cabin dates all the way back to ancient times and well before sawmills. The family was now definitely in the Appalachia. They were now primitive mountain people of Kentucky.

Heban was always completely disgusted with Max. Max had to learn all of this, and he really was trying his best. But Heban gave him no slack and no learning curve. Heban would yell and punch him and call him stupid day and night.

Heban made all the calculations and measurements

for the precise size of the logs. It was up to Max to cut the logs according to Heban's measurements. The measurements that Heban took ended up being wrong, and their ceiling inside the cabin ended up being only six feet tall. Of course, Heban did not take the blame for this big mistake. He blamed Max for the whole thing.

Heban had a habit of stabbing Max with his used syringes, and sometimes, he used his syringe as a dart to throw at any of the kids. That is except Jacob. When asked why he would do such a thing, he would laugh and say, "Because I just want to see how good my aim is." To this day, Max jumps when someone throws anything. It is an automatic reflex for him. He flinches, and then he ducks.

Heban's father always called Evelyn names and disrespected her. He would tell her that his son could have done better than her. One day when Jacob was about five or six and Heban and Evelyn were gone, the grandfather got drunk. Jacob said something the grandfather did not like, and he picked up a water hose and hit Jacob on his back and gave him a big welt. Jacob was scared and started crying. This made Max so angry when he saw what happened; he went over and punched the grandfather in the face and accidentally broke his nose. As soon as Heban and Evelyn returned home, the grandmother told Heban that Max hit his dad and broke his nose. Heban never asked why Max had done this, and he did not really care. He was going to teach Max a lesson with a beating he would never forget.

Things never changed, and the abuse continued to happen in Kentucky. Max was seventeen, and he was at the end of his rope with living like this.

After coming to the decision that he would not take this anymore, he went to school one day with a plan. Running away was not an option because they would just hunt you down and drag you back. Max had decided to ask a friend if after school was out, would he please drive him to the next town to talk with a recruiter about joining the Marines. Max spoke with a Sargent who told him he thought he would make a good Marine but that there was one problem. Max was only seventeen, and he would need his parent's permission. Max explained that his stepdad did not have custody, and he was sure his mom would sign. The Sargent said that would work, and he would be at Max's house at 6:00 p.m. that night.

When Max got home, he sat his mom down and told her about his decision and that the Sargent was coming at 6:00 p.m. Evelyn asked him why and Max said to her, "If I don't get out of here, I am going to kill Heban. I love you, Mom, but you have to sign, or when I turn eighteen, I'll leave, and I will never come back."

Evelyn signed that night, and after the Sargent left, Heban turned to Max and said, "Well, one thing for sure, you won't make it; you will fail. You are no good, you are lazy, and you are stupid."

Soon after, Max left for the Marines and did his testing, which was in Louisville, Kentucky. Max is still proud of himself. He scored extremely high in his aptitude. This high scoring opened the door for choosing many jobs, such as a computer tech and some other promising choices. But one option really stood out. He wanted to be an air traffic controller. It turned out Max was not stupid at all, even though Heban had told him that he was almost every day of his life.

Max was still home with his family through Christmas and left for Paris Island, SC, for basic training right after the holidays. It was extremely hard saying goodbye to his sisters and mother. He had nothing to say to Heban at all.

Max came home again three months later after completing basic training to see his mom and sisters. This visit infuriated Heban. Heban said to Max, "So you think you are all big and tough!" and then he drew back his fist to punch Max. Max shoved Heban back hard and said to him, "I'm done with you. If you hit me or my mom or my sisters, I'm going to defend myself and them." Heban was mad, and he yelled for Evelyn to get in the living room with them and said, "I want Max out of my house. He is telling me what I can and can't do." Max stood taller and said, "I'm not afraid of you anymore. This is done." For the next thirty days that Max was there while on his military leave, Heban did not touch anyone. After all the years of abuse, standing up to Heban gave Max a huge sense of relief. Max said, "Every dog has his day."

Basic training was tough, and there were days he questioned if he could make it. But Max was determined because he had to make it. When it was hard, he would say to himself that Heban was wrong about him. Even if he almost died trying, he was going to make it. He would prove Heban was wrong.

It was the month of March, and Max was on base. He knew Heban was still beating his mom, but on this day, Max had an overwhelming feeling that something was wrong. Max called home to check on her. Evelyn answered the phone, and she was crying. Max asked her what was wrong and if she was okay. Evelyn told Max that she had smashed her finger. He knew with every fiber in his body that she was not telling him the truth. Something snapped in him, and he said, "I'm calling the airport, and I am booking a flight, and I'm coming home." Evelyn begged him not to come and told him it would only make things worse. She said, "Promise me you won't come home." Max started to cry when they hung up, and he went back to his room and called the airport and booked a flight. He booked the very next flight out. He needed to get to the airport within the hour. He told his commanding officer he had a family emergency, and they gave him a few days leave. He needed a ride to the airport, so he offered a buddy $50.00 to take him right then. When the plane landed, he paid for a taxi ride all the way there and up the holler to the house.

It was around 8:30 or 9:00 p.m. when Max walked through the door of the house, and no one knew he was coming. Max walked in, and Heban was sitting in his chair. Evelyn saw Max and asked, "What on earth did you do?" Heban, yelling from his chair, said, "What does that little *sob* want?" With that, Max walked straight over to where Heban was sitting and punched him as hard as he could. Evelyn started crying and said, "Please stop. You are going to tear the house up." Heban started swinging his crutch at

Max. Heban had been using a crutch to help him walk. His abuse of narcotics and other health problems had started to affect him. Max said to Heban, "Let's take this outside." Heban boasted, "Sure; I know how this is going to end." Heban took a swing with his crutch at Max and missed him, and when he did, Max knocked him on the ground and kept punching him with every ounce of power that he had. He was punching Heban so hard that it scared Evelyn, and she called her daughters to come to the house to help. When Max finally stood back up and backed away, he said to Heban, "If I find out ever again that you hit my mother, I'll be back."

After about three years in the Marines, Max started having nightmares. He also started failing at some of his duties. He was not caring properly for his uniform, and he was doing poorly in school. His Master Sergeant called him into the office to have a talk. He said to Max, "I don't know what is going on with you, but your bunkmates are telling me you are mumbling in your sleep and screaming out at times. I would like you to see our staff psychiatrist to help to get to the bottom of this."

Max met with the psychiatrist, and after the fourth or fifth visit, he told the doctor about his childhood. He told him about the abuse, both sexual and physical. That his stepfather had tried to run him over with the tow wrecker truck, tied him to a pole in the basement several times, tried to drown him, beat him every day of his life with whips, hoses, belts, and then poured salt in his wounds after the beating. He went on. That his sisters and mother suffered most of this too. Max had decided he was going to let it all out. It had been bottled up all his life because you could not tell anyone. The threat was always there. If you tell, your mother will go back to prison, and you and your siblings will go to the orphanage. Finally, he thought this was a safe place, a confidential place for him to tell the truth about what had happened.

The doctor leaned back in his chair and said, "Son, when you want to tell me the truth about what actually really happened, we can move on. This cannot be true, no way. No child could survive what you have described. When you decide to tell the truth, you come back to see me." Max never went back. He felt the doctor was pompous and arrogant and had made matters worse by accusing Max of lying.

Max became friends with a Sergeant and a Lance corporal, and they spent some quality time together. They went fishing, golfed together, and Max joined them at their church. After church, he would be invited to go to one of their houses for dinner. Max struggled with the church and believing in God. He heard about God but had never believed there really was a God. He questioned why, if God were real why He would have allowed him, his mother, and his siblings to suffer as they did. He was told God loves you. For Max, it did not feel like God loved him at all.

Max spent twelve years in the Marines. Towards the end of his career, his exercise asthma worsened, and he was unable to complete most of his physical requirements as a marine. Because of this, he was medically discharged. This chapter in his life was over.

CHAPTER TWENTY-SIX

MAX FINDS GOD

After the service, Max was working in a warehouse and was making a mess out of his life. He had a few failed marriages, and he had started using drugs.

One day he was driving his car, and he saw a guy beating up on a girl on the side of a building. Max turned his car around and got out of it. He went up to the guy and started punching him and yelling at him for hitting the girl. The police were called, and the girl told the police that Max was trying to help her, so they did not arrest him that time. This would not be the only time this happened. After this first incident, there was more of the same. In all the incidents that followed the first one, he was arrested and then charged for assault. Max had a lot of pent-up anger, and every time he saw a guy beating a girl or a woman or a child, he would go to their rescue, and he would beat the guy up. He was arrested for this eight or nine times. Every time that he went to court, he had the same judge. The first time the judge asked him why he had done this, and Max explained it was because the guy was beating a defenseless girl. Max told the judge that he could not stand to see a grown man beating and abusing a woman or child. He said, "Judge, a woman is not a punching bag." The judge said, "I admire you for that young man, but you have to learn to control yourself." Three weeks later, he was back in court. This time the woman he helped was in court and asked the judge not to put Max in jail. She said, "Judge, no man has ever stepped in to help me. This is the best thing anyone's ever done for me." The judge this time said he would drop the charges but that he hoped he would never see Max again.

Within six months, Max was back in court for the same thing, and then five more times. The judge warned Max that this was it. He told him if he was in his court one more time, he was going to sentence him to jail time. He told Max that he was a vigilante without a weapon. He also said, "I understand why you are doing it, but as a judge, I must uphold the law. I repeat, he said, one more time, and you are going to jail."

A month later, Max was pulling into Walmart and saw on the side of the building a guy beating a girl. He whipped his car around, jumped out, and started punching the guy to get him to stop. Someone called the police. Max felt someone grab him from behind, and he turned around and punched him, and it was a cop. He had no idea. This was an assault on an officer this time, even though Max did not have any idea it was the police grabbing him from behind. He thought it might be a friend of the guy that was beating up the girl.

In court, the judge said, "Max, you went way beyond this time, and you hit an officer." Max told the judge that there were a lot of circumstances involved here. He explained he did not know it was a policeman and that he has too much respect for the police, and he would never knowingly hit or disrespect them. Max had a public defender, and he called the policeman to testify. He asked if the policeman had identified himself and the policeman admitted that he could not remember if he had or not. He was just trying to stop Max from hitting the guy. The judge said to the policeman, "If you cannot remember, then I am going to say that you did not identify yourself."

Max describes this day as the day God was sitting in this courtroom. The judge called for a fifteen-minute recess. The man that Max had beat up on the side of the store that day was in the courtroom. During the recess, he started taunting Max, saying, "Man, you are going to rot in jail." Max told him he did not care and that he needed to be the one to be worrying because there were a lot more guys that would beat him up if he kept beating up on women.

When the judge came back in the courtroom, he had Max stand and then said to him, "I have never met someone like you, and I admire you for protecting women and children. But I told you if you showed up here one more time, you were going to jail. I am dropping the charges on the officer, but I am going to uphold the assault on the other guy. You have to learn."

Suddenly, the doors at the back of the courthouse opened, and a woman came walking in, and she was crying. The judge asked her if she was okay and was she in the wrong place. The woman replied, "I need to talk to you judge, I need to talk to you about this guy standing in front of you. I do not know this guy but what I want to say before you send this man to jail is that the reason the other man here was beating me up was that I was pregnant, and he did not want the baby. So, he beat me bad enough that day that he killed my baby. All this guy Max did was try to save me and my baby." The judge looked shocked and responded by saying, "Do you have proof?" She responded that she did. "I have paperwork, your honor. I was four months pregnant." The judge read the paperwork that stated that due to the severe beating, she lost the baby. The judge looked up and spoke to the court and said to the bailiff, "Arrest that man," and he was pointing to the man that had beat her, "I'm charging him with murder." Then the judge turned his attention back to Max and said, "I was about to sentence you but honestly, what I want to tell you is that I wish you would have gotten to this poor woman sooner and saved her baby. You have a lot of integrity, and I respect you. The charges are dropped, and you are free to go." The woman then asked the judge if she could hug Max, that he was the only man that had ever stood up for her. The judge nodded and then said, "Once again by George, I wish you would have gotten there sooner."

After this, things went from bad to worse for Max, and he was really messing up. Besides the arrests for assault, he had a few failed marriages and a cocaine habit. Max had really lost his way since he left the service.

One night he was in a bar and met a girl who was sitting at the bar drinking. They struck up a conversation and ended up leaving together and then being together that night. Max saw her a few more times, but nothing became serious between them.

Max, sometime later over the next few months, met

someone he did fall in love with, and they married. What Max did not know right away was that his new wife's daughter was the same girl that he had met at the bar drinking one night and that he had been with. This awkward situation proved to be an explosive life-altering disaster for him. One night when Max's wife was working the second shift, the daughter approached Max in her mother's and his bedroom. Max told her to get out of the room and that what she was trying to do was wrong, to stop. She felt hurt and rejected. When Max had first met her in the bar, she was drinking. Max figured she was an adult of at least eighteen years old, or she would not have been able to buy drinks and sit at the bar. But unfortunately, at that time, she was only seventeen. Max rejecting her like he did and telling her that he loved her mother and to leave him alone was not what she wanted to hear. Max became more insistent and told her what she was trying to do was very wrong. This sent her into a hateful rage; she started yelling and screaming, and then she called the police. Max was also still on drugs at the time, which made things worse. Max was arrested and charged that very night with sodomy and child molestation.

Max had a public defender for his case. His attorney told him he was looking at three life sentences in the state

of Georgia, and he was never going to make it out of prison. It was at this time in Max's life, while sitting in jail
and facing a lifetime sentence to prison, that Max turned to
God. On his knees, praying and asking for God to please
help him in this very dark time. He turned to God, and God
answered him.

The next time his public defender came to talk with him
about his case, Max told him that he wanted him to make a
plea deal with the prosecuting attorney. Max said, "Tell the
prosecuting attorney I will do ten years in prison and ten
years' probation." Max said, "God told and showed me that
this should be my plea agreement and what I should ask
for." His public defender attorney responded with a shake
of his head, a smirk, and disgust on his face, and he called
Max a Bible thumper. He said to Max, "That ain't never
gonna happen." Max said, "I don't care. I want you to ask
for this plea agreement for me."

On June 2, Max's attorney came to see him at the jail.
The first thing the attorney said was, "I don't know who
you know or who your important contact is in the system,
but I don't appreciate being called at 3:00 a.m. in the morning and being told that I have to be down here to have you
sign the plea agreement. You got the ten years in prison and

ten years' probation." Max said, "Thank you, Lord." The attorney said, "Just sign it."

Life in prison for Max was a turning point in his life. Max said that when you feel like your life could not get any worse, God shines a bright light of hope on you and shows you the right path you need to take. This path became clear through a non-profit organization called Kiaros Prison Ministry International. The group is made up of several different denominations of churches and people. They come into prisons and have retreats and programs, dinners, fellowship, and sharing. From the very first time Max attended, he was blown away by all the positive feelings and the love and caring he felt. Max never missed any of the Kiaros' events, and soon, he became incredibly good friends with two men, Austin and Chuck, who were volunteers for the ministry.

Max shared his childhood story with Austin and Chuck. He wanted them to know where he had been and come from and where he hoped he could go with his life after he served his time. Max had never felt such genuine hope and compassion before, and he grew to be close friends with both.

As the years went by and Max was within six months

of being released, Austin and Chuck were still very much involved in serving the Lord and ministry and still friends with Max. Max shared with Austin that he did not know what to do when he got out. Austin said, "I'll be waiting for you outside these prison walls when you are released. I've seen how you have grown in the Lord." Max said, "But you live in Georgia, and all my family is in Kentucky."

As it turned out, Max was being released on Christmas Day, 2006. His interstate transfer and probation requirements for leaving the state of Georgia and moving to Kentucky had not yet been approved. He had to stay in Georgia until the processing was completed. Max told this to Austin. Austin said, "You will be coming home with me and my family until the paperwork processes." Max asked Austin, "Do you know what I was locked up for?" Austin replied, "I don't know, but what I do know is that God told me I can trust you. You may have done wrong, but all your past sins are forgiven. God set it on my heart to pick you up and take you to my home. It will be Christmas Day."

On the way to Austin's house, he stopped at Walmart to buy some clothes for Max. All he had was his prison clothes which anyone that would see him would know he had just gotten out of prison. Max told Austin that he did not have any money. Austin knew that, and he paid for a pair of shoes, jeans, and a nice shirt.

When they arrived at Austin's house, Austin's daughter greeted them at the door, Max stuck his hand out to shake hers and say hello, and the daughter said, "No shaking hands, I have a hug for you." Austin's wife had prepared a wonderful breakfast, and with all this, Max was starting to cry because he was overwhelmed by this family who was so kind and loving and cared about him. Little did Max know that he was about to have the best Christmas he had ever had in his entire life.

When Austin and his wife and daughter went into the living room to open gifts, Max hung back in the kitchen to let them open their gifts as a family. Austin asked Max what he was doing and to come into the living room and join them. Austin said to Max that he was part of their family now.

As Max sat there watching the daughter hand the gifts out, she looked over at Max and said, "We have some packages for you." Max received several presents from Austin and his family. Max was completely overwhelmed. While they were all enjoying this time together, Chuck called and told Max he would be picking him up soon to spend some time with him for Christmas. They went out to breakfast, so Max had two breakfast meals that day. After breakfast, Chuck took Max to his house, and there were more gifts for Max. Chuck then drove Max to another man's house, and his name was David. David's wife made dinner. After dinner, they surprised Max with a small box, and inside was a wallet and a keychain. Max said to them both, "God, it has been a long time since I carried a wallet and a key chain." David said, "Well, take it out of the box and open it up and see if you like it." When Max opened it up, it had three one hundred dollar bills in it. Max burst into tears. He was so totally taken back by the generosity of these three families. The love, the caring. He was overwhelmed by the fact that he had nowhere to go, and they took him in. This broken person who, through God's love and lots of prayers, had been given one of the greatest gifts, these three families.

Because it would take a few days for the probation paperwork to process, the three families covered the cost of a motel for Max. Before leaving Georgia, Max had to check in with the sheriff's department in the county. Austin drove him there. A sheriff deputy came walking out of one of the offices and said, "Max is that you? You finally out? Good for you!" He went on, "You know Max, they railroaded you; you did not deserve the sentence you got. They did not allow the evidence that would have proved your innocence. We had that proof, but the DA would not allow it."

Max's reaction was not at all what one would expect it to be. Max said, "Thank you, sheriff, for telling me that. But my going to prison was the best thing that could have happened to me. It got me off drugs, and I have found God, and I have peace. I have turned my life around, and I have made the best friends you could ever hope for in a lifetime." It almost left the sheriff speechless until he said, "I hope that the rest of your life is the absolute best of your life. Good luck."

Finding God and having the friendship with Austin and Chuck helped with the healing that Max needed. He had been avoiding his sisters because he thought they hated him for the things he was made to do with them by Heban. Through God's love, he learned they did not blame him. They knew he was forced to do it. Today they all have an unbreakable bond.

Max shares that we serve an awesome God. He puts all his life decisions in God's hands. He knows that he is still here today, still living and breathing because of God. Without God, he most likely would have been still serving three life sentences in prison.

Still today, Max is good friends and stays in contact with Chuck and Austin.

Thanks be to God for putting wonderful people like them in the ministry. Max tears up whenever he talks about them.

CHAPTER TWENTY-SEVEN

MORE TO COME— THE CURSE IS BROKEN

This is not the end of this story. This is not the final chapter. The lives of my cousins, my family, our children, and grandchildren are still very much here, growing, living, and loving.

What is different is the generational family curse has been broken. The curse that our mothers grew up with and lived. From the time they were just little girls and lost their mom, their lives were filled with years of violence, poverty, a stock market crash, wars, the depression, the holocaust, years of abuse, and sadness.

The curse was harder on Evelyn, the younger sister. After losing her mother and growing up with her stepmother, her self-esteem was crushed. She was made to feel homely and unworthy. She left home at age sixteen and had two bad marriages. She lost her kids to foster care, went to prison, and suffered physical abuse and mental abuse every day of her life until her second husband, Heban, died. She witnessed and felt the pain that her children suffered at the hands of her second husband, Heban. She suffered mentally and physically because she was unable to save and protect her children or herself from the years of abuse.

Evelyn lived to be seventy-six years old. Out of those seventy-six years, the happiest years for her were the eleven years she spent with her children after Heban died. Seventy percent of her life was spent being unhappy and abused. She had no control over the situation, and she lived in constant fear. Fear that she would lose her children again and she would go back to prison. The alternate fear was being beaten to death by her husband.

No more, her children chide! No more suffering! No more abuse! It stops here! The curse is broken!

Are Evelyn's children scarred and traumatized by all that they suffered? Yes, they most definitely are! They are fragile. But they are not broken. Each of them has more love and compassion for others than one could think is even possible. The determination and strength that each of them has is worthy of extremely high praise.

Their love and faith in God are what make them stronger. They are humble. Their unselfishness towards others is above and beyond. They are prayer warriors for the sick and disadvantaged. They always sincerely wish for the absolute best for others.

One of their biggest hopes by speaking out is to bring attention to the foster care system. To find a way to make the powers more aware that our system is flawed and fails many of our children. They know and remember the pain and suffering they endured as kids many years ago. Still, today, they hear and see some of the same abuses in foster care homes. They know of children within their own communities being beaten, going to bed hungry, feeling afraid, and feeling hopeless. The siblings feel that they are without the power to make positive changes for these children. But they feel that if they speak out about the abuse and keep spreading the word, it will make many others aware. This speaking out would hopefully motivate the powers to help make a change. If this speaking out helps just one child, it is a positive move towards ending a living nightmare for a child. It is their belief that many people become foster parents for the monetary benefits and not for the care and genuine compassion for a foster child. The reason many of these children are in foster care, to begin with, is to take them away from their parents and a bad situation in their home. Many of these children are taken out of one bad situation and sometimes placed in an even worse situation. This was the case for Evelyn's children.

Not all foster care parents and homes are bad. That is not the message. But one would hope that there could be more homes out there like Nancy's foster care home. She loved her foster care parents, and they showered her with love too.

Katie is a proud mother and grandmother. She is very caring and loving. She has worked hard most of her life, is smart, and has accomplished much, but now her health has started to fail. She still acts like a mother hen to her younger sisters and brothers. She has lots of compassion for others. She has never forgiven herself for not being able to do more to protect her siblings from all the abuse. She always felt, as the oldest child, that it was her responsibility to protect them even though she was just a child herself. She went to great lengths and great monetary expenses as an adult to try and protect her mother and sisters. She stood up to Heban, which very few ever had. She grew stronger and braver through the years. Her faith in God and his love surrounds her.

She lacks understanding of why her mother did not do more to protect and save her children. As a mother and grandmother herself, it is hard for her to understand. But she is accepting of the answer being that her mother was just too afraid. Not strong enough. Her mother had been beaten down all her life.

Nancy is what you would call a scrapper. You can knock her down, but by golly, she is going to get back up if it takes every ounce of strength that she has in her. She was quite successful in her career life, moving up the ladder to management. She is very independent, smart, and resourceful. She is a loving mother and grandmother and is very much still in love with her soul mate.

She did not have nice things as a child; she was embarrassed by it and was unhappy. Because of this, she always goes above and beyond for her family. She herself will do without if she must just to be able to give to them. Nancy loves her family so much and wants their life to be so much better than hers. This is what is most important to her.

Nancy is a pillar of strength and someone you would want to have on your team. She is loyal and dependable, and smart. She can be tough on the outside when pushed too far but very loving on the inside. She would give you the shirt off her back and expect nothing in return. Her faith in God is unwavering. She takes everything to God.

She has some stomach issues that knock the wind out of her sails, but she only allows that to temporarily keep her down. She wills herself to get back up. She always pushes herself to the limit.

She loved her mom but always had a part of her that lacked understanding about why her mom did not protect her children. She feels just like Katie that if either of them was in her shoes that they would have done more to protect their children.

Max has suffered an extremely hard life for almost all his life. It is most difficult to understand how it is possible that he has turned out to be such a great guy. He is the first to pick up the phone and say, "I love you. I will pray for you. How can I help you?" To have been severely beaten and abused and still not be completely broken. To not be hateful and resentful. That he is not. Kindness and love are something he wears on his sleeve. He is a blessing to others and someone you would want to have in your corner when you feel like you cannot go on anymore.

Max still rocks in his bed at night. Maybe it is because, in the darkness, he is reminded of his tortures and pain. It is not talked about.

He is not stupid as he was told that he was by Heban for

so many years. He has a remarkably high aptitude and is skilled at almost any project or job that he takes on. He is a protector of his siblings, loves his wife and family, and his faith in God guides his daily life. He feels he has so much to be thankful for.

Maria was timid and afraid growing up. There was a lot she did not understand because her life was so distorted at such an early age. After going into foster care, she did not really remember her mother the day she came for her. She did not understand what life was like for other children. What she did know was she did not like the life she had. Her sister Nancy tutored her to be stronger along the way. Nancy felt she had to, or Maria would not have been able to survive. Their life with the physical and sexual abuse was just too hard. Nancy knew she had to help her find a way to hold on.

Maria has been married to her husband for many years now. They have three beautiful young daughters and grandchildren. They have a beautiful home. Her husband is a good provider and a hard worker, and Maria has a successful career herself. Maria and her husband have a deep respect for each other, and they never argue and fight. Her old life filled with screaming and yelling and beatings is over for her.

Maria did not make it to fulfill her dream of becoming a flight nurse, but she does have a job where she works with people and their loved ones. Her compassion for her job and helping others is felt by everyone that knows her. She is very well respected and depended on.

If you need a protector, you might want to call on Maria. If you need someone to pray for you, encourage you, offer to help you, know that you can count on her to be there for you. Smart, strong, and faithful. Having faith in God and taking everything to him in prayer is how she lives her life.

Maria's understanding is her mom wanted to help and protect her kids and she did step in to try and stop the abuse many times. She feels that her mother's biggest fear was losing her kids again. Her mother worried about being separated and going back to prison. It was a no-win situation. Damned if you do, damned if you do not.

Cynthia is a very warm, gentle, and loving person. She is very emotional about how people treat each other. She finds comfort in being able to share with others how to deal with some of the evil ways in the world. The foster care abuse is a big concern for her too.

She becomes very afraid of anyone yelling and loud voices. She would rather be hit than be yelled at. She is also afraid of people throwing things, even if it is just for fun. It brings up the memory of Heban throwing work boots and other objects at the kids to hurt them.

There was so much she had to hide and lie about as a kid growing up and going to school. She felt so unprotected because you could not ask for help. She really loved her real dad. Even though he was a drinker and a womanizer, at least, she felt that he really did love her. Love from a parent was something she felt truly little of ever having while living with Heban and her mother.

Cynthia has a way about her that you can feel close to her after only talking for a few minutes. That is why the little girl who was severely burned in the fire that Cynthia made friends with knew she had met the best possible friend for her. "Lonely Girl," as Cynthia was called back in school, has a big heart.

Elizabeth, my mother, and the oldest sister left this world after suffering several years in a nursing home with Alzheimer's. Life in the nursing home was a struggle for her. She was used to being the boss. When her sister Evelyn's children came to visit her at the nursing home a few years before she died, they were shocked by how she looked. They had never seen their aunt Elizabeth without makeup, a beautiful hairstyle, and nicely dressed. Here at the nursing home, she had a buster brown haircut, sweatpants, and a stained sweatshirt from spilling her food on it. They were in total disbelief at how she looked and acted. They felt like this could not possibly be the aunt they adored. Each of the sisters remarked that if Elizabeth had known what she looked like, she would have been madder than a wet hen. She had never been to visit them in Kentucky without always being nicely dressed and her hair perfectly styled. They thought she was classy.

Elizabeth did not even know who they were when they visited. But by this time, she really did not even know her own children most of the time. People just looked familiar to her, and she would smile and say she loved them. She seemed to always remember her niceties. "Hello, how are you? I love you, goodbye."

When Elizabeth and Daniel started traveling to Florida for the winter after Elizabeth retired, they always made a special point to stop and visit her dad, stepmother, her sister, and her nieces and nephews in Kentucky. She and her sister were not ever close, but Elizabeth did enjoy seeing the kids. She made an extra effort to see her dad, but her stepmother always said something mean and hurtful that would cut the visit short. Many a time, Elizabeth and Daniel stormed out of the house and out of the holler.

Elizabeth and Evelyn were always pitted against each other by their stepmother. The stepmother always enjoyed stirring the pot. Mildred, the stepmother, would spin wild stories and accusations that were not true, and this kept the two sisters from being close and put them at odds with each other. Evelyn was always jealous of Elizabeth. Rightfully so. Evelyn had nothing but huge distortions and lies to brag about. Her life was on a very dark path.

Elizabeth's childhood got off to a rough start, and her first marriage certainly had its struggles too. Owen's epilepsy and mental struggles caused years of hard times and abuse for Elizabeth and her children. After Owen died, Elizabeth started to grow as an independent woman. She had new hope and a bright new picture for her life.

The times that Daniel and Elizabeth traveled and lived in Florida were some of the happiest times in both of their lives. She loved and adored her family and grandchildren and was home for the holidays. But she loved all the friends and activities and lifestyle that Daniel and she shared in

Florida.

My husband and I made a point to spend at least one week of our vacation each year to visit my mom and Daniel in Florida. This was a huge pride and joy for Elizabeth and Daniel to boast about. They were so proud that their daughter and son-in-law would want to spend time with them and their friends. Elizabeth and Daniel showed us off to everyone they knew. It was a lot of fun for myself and my husband too. Together, we played golf, went dancing, sang karaoke, and went out to eat.

Somehow in the years ahead and along the way, Elizabeth and Daniel said that they were made to feel guilty about being away from the grandkids so much. They decided to sell their much nicer place in Florida. They bought a used trailer back in Ohio to live in for the winter months. They then bought a smaller trailer and put it on a lot in Florida. There were lots of promises between everyone about spending more time together when they were in Ohio, but that was not the reality. The grandkids were getting older, and the parents were busy working and doing their own thing. There was always a bit of regret by Elizabeth and Daniel about this decision and the change that they had made.

On one of the visits to Florida, I talked to my mom's friends about mom's failing memory. I also observed my mother for myself, and it was obvious my mother was rapidly declining. She did not care about getting her hair done or dressing up. She did not want to work on her computer. She was not taking care of the finances anymore. All of this was concerning, so I made an appointment to have her tested for Alzheimer's and dementia. Unfortunately, the diagnosis was confirmed that she did have Alzheimer's. Medications were prescribed for her, along with follow-up appointments. Unfortunately, neither Elizabeth nor Daniel remembered or kept any of the future appointments for her. They forgot about staying on the medications too. It was an unfortunate mistake. My learning about this was not until months later. We were miles apart. They were in Florida, and I was back home in Ohio. There were phone calls but no indication that they were missing appointments and not filling prescriptions.

Alzheimer's is such an awful disease. It robs the person that is suffering from it, and it robs everyone around them. At the time that all of this was happening, Daniel had received news that he had lost his summer part-time grass cutting job back in Ohio. This job had helped to supplement their income, and they had been relying on this money for a long time. Money was getting tighter, and within a year after Elizabeth's diagnosis, they had to file bankruptcy. They would not be able to go back to Florida because their home there was being repossessed.

This news was a crushing blow for them. It was also a terrible embarrassment. Elizabeth seemed to take this the hardest. She enjoyed everything about their life there. She felt Ohio was lonely with the family so busy, and she missed the structured activities she did in Florida.

It seemed at this time for her that she had nothing to look forward to and did not care anymore. She was giving up all hope. She would walk from room to room in their trailer, repeating over and over that she wanted to be in Florida. There was nothing you could say to her to make her feel better. She was both sad and angry. There was some discussion that possibly my brother and I could figure something out so they could spend some time in Florida. This was a big no for Daniel. It was terribly embarrassing for Daniel that they had to file bankruptcy. It hurt his pride. Their trailer was repossessed, and all their friends in the park knew this. A big rig showed up one day at the park office where they lived. The driver of the rig provided proof to the manager that their home was being repossessed. Daniel pictured what this must have looked like and what people might be saying. They were still their friends with most of the people in the park, but it was different now. Elizabeth continued to be on a rapid decline with her health, so the kids' discussions about all this stopped. Unfortunately, Elizabeth did not stop. She continued to sob, walking room to room and repeating how much she missed it there.

Looking back over their life, Daniel and Elizabeth had a good run. They had several years of good times. Daniel was always about fun, and together, they had made many close friends. They had squeezed in and made some great memories. They enjoyed a lot of the same things when it came to special interests and activities. They made a good match.

After the bankruptcy, life grew bleaker for both. Elizabeth blamed Daniel, and Daniel blamed her. They seemed to grow a bit apart. Alzheimer's magnified all of this.

One day when I stopped to visit them, Daniel told me that my mother had not eaten in a week. I had just returned from a business trip. Meals on Wheels had been bringing meals in for them, and mom claimed that she did not like their food. I jumped in the car and ran to the nearest fast-food restaurant and got her a milkshake, fries, and a hamburger. Her eyes lit up when I returned. This was the kind of food she liked. She was hungry, and she ate all of it right away. This was concerning that she had not eaten in a week, and soon I became increasingly worried about her care. Maybe some changes needed to be made. I decided to call my brother to talk about all of this. We needed to be sure she was eating right, and perhaps we needed some supervised care for her.

Soon Elizabeth started wandering away from home. Daniel would be taking a nap and find that she was gone when he woke up. It became more important to look for a nursing home with round-the-clock care. Somewhere that also specialized in memory care and Alzheimer's. I was still working full time so taking mom to my house was not the best option.

The big difference between the sisters Elizabeth and Evelyn was that Elizabeth's life had about thirty good years. She got to travel, have friends, and have a successful career. She became more independent, confident, stronger, and determined as she got older. She worked hard, made good money, and knew how to have a good time. She let go of the hurt and memory of being unworthy and being made to feel that being the daughter of a pig farmer was somehow bad. It wasn't. All the mean things that her stepmother did and said to her. Elizabeth knew she could be more. She could have more. She was strong and determined.

It is no wonder that her sister Evelyn felt a little jealous. Evelyn had a life of lack and misery. And the stepmother was quick to remind her that she had never amounted to anything, just like she had told her growing up. The hand-writing was on the wall.

Before Evelyn passed away, she and Elizabeth mended some of their differences and became a little closer. By this time, their dad and stepmother had passed away. Both sisters were attending church and putting more of their life in God's hands.

It was easy to be upset with Daniel and blame him when Elizabeth, my mom, was not eating right and wandering off. That coupled with the financial difficulties they were having and running out of money. Plenty of times, they had to call for help to buy groceries and others. It had to be hard on Daniel to see Elizabeth fading far away from him. Elizabeth had always been so strong and handled almost everything. So, looking back now, I feel bad that I was disappointed. I know being a caretaker for someone with Alzheimer's is a hard struggle.

It was not until after both Daniel and Elizabeth had

passed on that I started reflecting on my mother's life, and I started seeing things differently. When I started learning more about her life growing up through spending time with my cousin's my feelings really changed. I learned how bad Evelyn's life and her children's life really were. Our talks and spending time really put a lot of things into perspective. How could I possibly fault Daniel? In comparison to Evelyn, my mother had lived like a queen while married to Daniel. He never beat her, he loved her, he made her laugh. Having him in her life gave her many years of happiness. Even if they had financially invested in one too many bad business decisions. They say it is always better to have tried and failed than to not have even tried at all. Daniel and Elizabeth had a special bond and love. Not to say they did not have arguments and disagreements because they did. So many times, as children, we cannot see and understand a lot of things about our parents. If they were both here now, I would say, "Well done, so happy for the both of you." Before Daniel died, he told me that he was not sorry for any of the decisions that he had made in life. That he felt he had lived a good life. I was glad that he left this world feeling that way and was at peace with himself. A lot of people have regrets about the things they never achieved or accomplished. Before my mom's Alzheimer's took away all of her memory, she would ask me when I came to visit her at the nursing home, "Where is my lover?" Her eyes would twinkle when she said it. I remember how special I thought it was to hear her say that. She still remembered him, and it reminded me how much she loved Daniel.

I know now having Daniel in her life, after so many hard years before him, was like finding her four-leaf clover.

POSTSCRIPT

Jesus said, "He who is without sin can cast the first stone."

Now, what does that mean? Why is this important?

This passage tells us that we do not accuse others unless we search our own hearts and minds to make certain we are pure (Matthew 7:3).

I grow tired of being around people who are quick to judge others and dig up any possible infraction and past wrong to put someone in a bad light to make themselves look better.

It happens at work. It happens at school. It happens at home, sporting events, everyday life.

And there are those that will lie to try and control an outcome.

I pray, dear Lord, that for each of us, including those that are reading this page right now, to remember Jesus is the only sinless person.

When any of us attempt to make others look bad, judge others, and gossip about their past mistakes, this is seen and heard by God and noted.

Lord, help us to be better in all that we do and more forgiving of others. Help us to share more about the love of Jesus and not share about other people's past mistakes.

Let us pray more and join and work together to make our world a better place.

BIBLIOGRAPHY

The Agricultural Adjustment Administration and the New Deal, 1933. Berkeley: University of California Press, 1969.

Vann, Mick. *The Austin Chronicle. The History of Pigs in America.* April 10, 2009.

Britannica. "Buchenwald Concentration camp, Germany."

Britannica. "Stock Market Crash of 1929 American History."

History. "Bombing of Hiroshima and Nagasaki."

Scheid, M, Jeanette. *Children in Foster Care: Issues and Concerns.* In *Psychiatric Times*, Vol 33 No 6, Volume 33, Issue. June 29, 2016.

Wikipedia. "The Diary of a Young Girl."

The Epilepsy Center of Northwest Ohio, Inc. "Education & Awareness & Treatment Options."

History. "FDR's First Inaugural Address Declaring 'War" on the Great Depression." October 14, 2009.

History. "Great Depression History."

Remembering 1965 Palm Sunday Tornado. Published April 5, 2015, Toledo Blade.

History. "The Roaring Twenties."

Carver, Joseph M. *Rocking Behavior in Children.*

The White House Publications. "John F. Kennedy."

Wikipedia. "Woodstock."

9 781637 697283